Evaluating the Superintendent

Evaluating the Superintendent

The Process of Collaborative Compromises and Critical Considerations

Jarett Powers
Constance D. Evelyn

ROWMAN & LITTLEFIELD
Lanham • Boulder • New York • London

Copublished with the School Superintendents Association

Published by Rowman & Littlefield
An imprint of The Rowman & Littlefield Publishing Group, Inc.
4501 Forbes Boulevard, Suite 200, Lanham, Maryland 20706
www.rowman.com

6 Tinworth Street, London SE11 5AL

Copyright © 2019 by Jarett Powers and Constance D. Evelyn

All rights reserved. No part of this book may be reproduced in any form or by any electronic or mechanical means, including information storage and retrieval systems, without written permission from the publisher, except by a reviewer who may quote passages in a review.

British Library Cataloguing in Publication Information Available

Library of Congress Cataloging-in-Publication Data

Names: Powers, Jarett, 1982–, author. | Evelyn, Constance D., 1967–, author.
Title: Evaluating the superintendent : the process of collaborative compromises and critical considerations / Jarett Powers and Constance D. Evelyn.
Description: Lanham : Rowman & Littlefield, [2019] | Includes bibliographical references.
Identifiers: LCCN 2019010821 (print) | LCCN 2019013961 (ebook) | ISBN 9781475849837 (electronic) | ISBN 9781475849813 (cloth   ) | ISBN 9781475849820 (pbk.   )
Subjects: LCSH: School superintendents—Rating of—United States.
Classification: LCC LB2831.762 (ebook) | LCC LB2831.762 .P68 2019 (print) | DDC 371.2/011—dc23
LC record available at https://lccn.loc.gov/2019010821

Contents

Foreword		vii
Acknowledgments		ix
Introduction		xi
1	The Relationship: How It Starts Is How It Ends	1
2	Institutional Memory	25
3	Communication, Communication, Communication: Mind the Gap	41
4	"Standard" of Leading	55
5	Solstice	81
Epilogue: Evaluating the Superintendent		99
References		101
About the Authors		107

Foreword

I was honored when Jarett Powers and Constance Evelyn, a member of the National Superintendents Roundtable, asked me to review this new book. *Evaluating the Superintendent* is a guide that will help board members and superintendents improve the crucial and tricky process of making judgments about superintendents' success. As school leaders find themselves increasingly under a microscope, this contribution could not come at a better time.

Connie Evelyn and Jarett Powers bring two distinct and important perspectives to bear on this issue. Evelyn, Valley Stream superintendent of schools, serves in densely populated Nassau County near JFK airport, and Powers is the Union Springs superintendent in the sparsely populated Finger Lakes region of central New York. These different perspectives make this a valuable text that can and should be used by districts large and small.

While the book is framed around the crucial issue of evaluation, it is really about how districts, school boards, and superintendents can succeed in their important work while using evaluation protocols to drive improvement. In that sense, it is at least as much about elevating district performance as it is about evaluating the superintendent.

Timothy Healy, a legendary president of Georgetown University, used to like to say that a university board had only two functions: hire the president and fire the president! (Anything else is meddling.) As we all know, that is not true of school boards, who are policymakers, and superintendents, who lead the district and carry out board mandates.

But there is a certain similarity. It is what happens between the beginning and the end of the relationship that nurtures or impedes a superintendent's success. This book addresses the following:

- Some of that similarity with higher education is captured in the title of chapter 1: "The Relationship: How It Starts Is How It Ends." A superintendent and board who cannot agree on what they are trying to accomplish at the outset are leaving themselves in for a rocky ride.
- Chapter 2 focuses on institutional memory and the sometimes complicated dance a new superintendent has to perform in terms of respecting the best of the district's past while moving it toward the future.
- Communication, communication, communication is the theme of chapter 3, with the timeless admonition that job #1 is "No surprises!" That is to say, no surprises for the board and no surprises for the community.
- Chapter 4 addresses the standard of leadership. Reminiscent of the distinction between technical and adaptive challenges described by Harvard's Ronald A. Heifetz in *Leadership without Easy Answers*, this is the difference between transactional and transformational challenges.
- Finally, chapter 5 points to the need for an ongoing process of carefully approached and structured change, organized around a vision of the district's aspirations. It starts with an entry plan, proceeds through communication and administrative protocols, and ensures that the evaluation process is deliberate and thoughtful, not something rushed through at the end of the contract year.

Everyone likes change, as a wag once put it, as long as everyone else changes. As the authors note, change cannot be foisted on a district. Shared understandings between the central office, the board, teachers, and the community are formidable resources in the search for improvement. Efforts to take shortcuts to these understandings are not likely to end well.

Best of all in this useful little volume are the examples and stories of the fiendishly deceptive traps and snares lying await every day for the unprepared superintendent. These illustrations alone make the book worthwhile. They can provide grist for role playing and professional development to help superintendents and board members alike.

—James Harvey, executive director
National Superintendents Roundtable

Acknowledgments

Superintendents have persisted over time to create new pathways for student success through their dedicated leadership across decades of educational reform. As twenty-first-century leaders, we are grateful to Rowman & Littlefield for their support of this text. We are also indebted to the many educators and board members that we have had the privilege of working shoulder to shoulder with to ensure that all students access equitable learning opportunities and outcomes.

Thank you to Jacinda Conboy, Tonie McDonald, Lesli Myers, Oliver Robinson, and Sharon Contreras for their insight and competence in reviewing this work. I am indebted to the Board of Education in Valley Stream Thirteen Union Free School District (UFSD) for their generous commitment of time and concentrated intellect as we continue on this transformative journey together. In particular, I want to thank my son, Keiro Luke, for his constant love and support. He is always with me.

—Constance Evelyn

Janet Abowd, Maryterese Pasquale-Bowen, and Janice White are leaders of learning and educators of the highest caliber and I thank them for their patience, support, and dedication to the craft of teaching. I am forever grateful to the Board of Education of Union Springs, who each day push me to grow and develop as a district leader.

—Jarett Powers

Introduction

Beginnings. The start of most things can hold much promise, giving us the chance to review our progress, contemplate forward thinking, and imagine critical outcomes as the result of diligent efforts. Beginnings bring with them new relationships, rich opportunities for reflection, and unique challenges to lead. Beginnings are also accompanied by trepidation of what lies ahead and questions, in our case of school districts, of how the board and superintendent as a singular entity will chart a course that positively affects the lives of all children. Shifting enrollment trends, efforts to conserve diminishing resources, and a desire to build on previous successes as an organization have led superintendents to this moment: the start of constructing a highly effective governance team.

The first moments of a superintendency are filled with urgency and emotion. What goals can be accomplished? How will people respond to new ideas and operational designs? What are the expectations for the district and its new leader? And how can a superintendent be quickly brought up to speed to direct the district's continuous improvement efforts?

All the energy and excitement that surrounds the beginning of a superintendency often blind both the board and the incoming superintendent to questions that must be immediately answered, even though the actual event is a year away: *How will the superintendent be evaluated?* and *What are the agreed-upon, measurable, and evidentiary indicators of efficacious performance that will ultimately anchor the evaluation process?*

The answer to the second question, if in fact it has been previously considered by districts, is typically answered with "custom and tradition." In some places the answer can be found in a summative narrative or checklist of indicators that may or may not be aligned with the current needs and goals of the district, depending on the nature of the search process for a new leader.

And yet superintendents begin the job of cultivating relationships with board members, developing communication protocols, generating innovative ideas, and leading through board agendas. They often undertake working with and managing the staff of the entire district without a clear understanding of the summative performance expectations of how their work will be evaluated. Either the board or the superintendent should clarify this ambiguity.

The test of considering this question is not revelational, and yet the research that undergirds some of the answers are often found to be anecdotal in nature. In contrast, accountability is always in the minds of the public, the board, and the superintendent. And, therefore, how do we effectively square this deal?

Accountability metrics and the public's perceptions of these measures have increasingly become a part of the dialogue about schools. Paired with these discussions is the political discourse about how to effectively measure the quality of teachers, building leadership, and schools across an array of perspectives and standards. What has yet to emerge is how to effectively evaluate the superintendent's role as it relates to the educational outcomes and overall success of school districts.

In a study designed for the Brookings Institute, Chingos, Whitehurst, and Lindquist (2014) found that there is no easy correlation between student performance and superintendent leadership. They held that because of the transient nature of the job, it is indeed the quality of classroom instruction that best determines the efficacy of a school district. Accordingly, school boards must grapple with how to assess the effectiveness of their school superintendent against a clouded threshold of both managerial and educational prerogatives. We contend that the superintendent plays a compulsory and central role in facilitating the evaluation process.

The school superintendent is more than a symbolic figure representing the educational interests of a community. The individual in service as the superintendent of schools is the district's educational leader and also acts as the chief executive officer who manages the day-to-day operations of what in most cases is a multimillion-dollar operation. This can fly in the face of established roles in more provincial localities that may have assumed a "mom and pop" approach toward running this enterprise.

The challenges involved in blending educational leadership with obligatory skill sets associated with the successful management of operations, financial and human capital, and the effective usage of data and technology is often represented in the board-superintendent dynamic (Kowalski 2005). This relational dynamic and the varied opinions of board members have the potential to become the basis of a superintendent's evaluation. How the superintendent is given feedback, guidance, and direction is in large part a reflection of how the district, through its elected representatives, perceives itself, assumes and identifies strategic goals, and ultimately measures success.

The tests and trials of leading public school districts have intensified the need for boards to authentically evaluate the highest administrative officer of the district. As noted by researchers, "participating in hiring a superintendent is one of the most important duties facing a school board member" (Sabatino 2010, xii). This book expands on this perspective and further posits that the superintendent's evaluation is the school board's vehicle to improve the ability of the superintendent to increase learning outcomes for all students.

This goal is often thwarted, however, by a lack of transparency and training relative to the school board's evaluation of the superintendent. The derailed value of this process can lead to power struggles and personality conflicts that reflect bereft understandings of the respective roles of board members and the superintendent. This book will provide insights and practical strategies for superintendents and board trustees to use to build a meaningful evaluation framework.

Focusing on process over substantive evaluatory content has been a historical trend in evaluating school superintendents (DiPaola & Stronge 2003). Understanding the evaluatory process as it currently exists and its relationship to the efficacy of standards and practices will refine the usefulness of the superintendent's evaluation, alignment of district-level leadership support, and measurable improvement for student achievement outcomes.

Moreover, managerial tasks have often been the mainstay in the evaluation of school superintendents, thereby limiting the focus on the role of the superintendent in leading curriculum, instruction, and assessment within a learning organization (DiPaola & Stronge 2003). DiPaola and Stronge's 2003 study (23) revealed further inconsistencies regarding superintendents' evaluations:

Although there is increasing consensus that assessment of student progress must be used in educational evaluation (Candoli et al. 1997), student learning alone does not capture the realm of public expectations nor does it capture the day-to-day realities of the responsibilities of school superintendents.

Evaluations establish a structured understanding between the superintendent and school board regarding expectations, desired longitudinal outcomes, and progress relating to district goals (Robinson & Bickers, 1990). While these expectations, outcomes, and progress metrics vary between school districts, the general reasons for developing them as part of the evaluation process are based on intentional practice. A wealth of literature has been developed in recent years regarding the importance of effectively evaluating teachers and school building leaders (Waters & Marzano 2006; Center for Educational Leadership 2015; Hallinger 2003). However, the literature regarding the superintendent's evaluation remains dated, underdeveloped, and in many instances written by school board members, superintendent search consultants, and practicing and retired school district leaders (Boyd 1966; Turner 1971; Bippus 1985; Braddom 1986).

As a result of the lack of formal contemporary studies regarding the evaluation of the superintendent, the arc of literature used for this book encompasses a broad swath of contributions. In addition, the content of this book is supported by the professional experiences of the authors.

The culture of accountability, as it is often perceived with regard to superintendent evaluations, has less to do with the superintendent's accountability to the board than it does the board's answerability to the various constituencies it serves. Because school boards feel compelled to justify their decision-making processes to key stakeholder groups, they must have data that supports their decisions, particularly with regard to renewing the superintendent's contract (Heller 1978).

Heller (1978, 5) also found that school boards come under greater pressure to justify their actions "as the increasing rapid turnover of superintendents, declining enrollments, scarcity of resources, changes in the public's attitude toward public education, which unfortunately are predicated upon suspicion, and a declining faith in the value of public education" heightens public scrutiny and provokes skepticism about public school leadership.

All these attributes have come to dominate the conversation surrounding public education. Consequently, superintendents' evaluations are a trifold exchange between school board members, their constituents, and the superintendent.

The idea that there are flaws in the evaluation process of the school superintendent as it is presently devised was argued by Candoli, Cullen, and Stufflebeam (1997, xi) when they wrote:

> Obvious deficiencies in present superintendent performance evaluations include insufficient focus on job-performance criteria, inadequately trained evaluators, weak evaluation model, and technically inadequate methods. Given the important purposes of superintendent performance evaluations, it is vital to correct these deficiencies.

While educators have come to expect that the standards of accountability mean being evaluated in the context of a given result, Mayo and McCartney's (2004, 19) study of 1,125 school superintendents found that when it comes to superintendents, the evaluatory criteria utilized focused more on personal dispositional characteristics than the "result-based criteria required of the latest accountability movement." Moreover, Mayo and McCartney found that most superintendents would not object to evaluations based on result-driven outcomes, but the current style and modalities of the board evaluation of the superintendent rarely allows for such an intentional process to take place.

Mayo and McCartney's (2004) findings are built on the work of Glass, Bjork, and Brunner (2000, 61), who found in their study of the school superintendency that:

> The belief by a significant number of superintendents that they are not being evaluated by criteria in their job descriptions reinforces the notion that the quality of the interpersonal relationships between the superintendent and board members is really what counts.

The superintendent and the board should have a good working relationship, but personal dynamics between members of the board and the superintendent should not dominate the foundation of the superintendent's evaluation. Conversely, strong personal relationships between the board and the superintendent should not mistakenly serve as a substitute for a formal evaluation. The need to avoid these and other missteps should serve as a reminder of the importance of having a cogent process capable of weathering such challenges.

Despite an increased focus on building a culture of accountability, the actual work and methodology necessary to have an effective evaluative process has for the most part not been developed at the school board–

superintendent level (Dillon & Halliwell 1991). Accordingly, in their study of New York State school superintendents and board presidents, Dillon and Halliwell established that the greatest dissonance between these parties was a mixed review of the purpose of board-level evaluations of the superintendent.

School board presidents in the study concluded that the central rationale for the evaluation was to improve the superintendent's instructional leadership of the district, but only one-eighth of school superintendents in the study identified increasing instructional leadership capacity as the primary objective of the evaluative process. Alternatively, school superintendents reflected that the driving objective of the evaluative process was to "strengthen the working relationship with the community and between the board of education and the superintendent" (Dillon & Halliwell 1991, 332).

The way to address the dissonance often found in the evaluation process is for the board to focus on accountability through sound policy related to the evaluation of the superintendent of schools (Foldesy 1989). Foldesy also contended that school boards must devise a methodology to take ambiguous state-level regulations and broaden them to meet the identified needs of the school district. He argued that if the purpose of superintendent evaluations is to improve student instruction, then the board must evaluate a superintendent's job performance in that domain.

This book will discuss how boards can leverage the development of policy and practice to highlight data points that inform the superintendent's evaluation, address who conducts the evaluation, and explain how to advance the narrative from a required employment agreement clause toward a more robust dialogue about how the superintendent is progressing as a leader—including recommendations for improvement (Foldesy 1989).

Seeing the superintendent as an individual whose primary job it is to advance instructional outcomes for students is a shift from the historical models of organizational management that have defined the superintendency. If instructional improvement is to be the driving impetus of the superintendency, managerial objectives must align to the desired outcomes surrounding instructional improvement. To develop this outcome-oriented mindset, the superintendent must work to define such goals with the school board within the given budgetary parameters and priorities, in partnership with the administrative staff of the district (Bjork 1993).

While the rationale behind evaluation theory is well established, little has been written about how boards and superintendents should approach the evaluation processes. Thus, the current wisdom regarding the operational alignment of the evaluation process to clearly defined standards, public transparency, and the contemporary purpose for conducting an evaluation is not well defined. This book seeks to fill that gap with practical strategies and key ideas based on authentic execution.

Chapter One

The Relationship

How It Starts Is How It Ends

On any given day, you can go to Google News and type in *School Superintendent Evaluation* to find a host of news articles highlighting the good, the bad, and the ugly relating to superintendents' evaluations. While some stories outline positive commendations and A+ ratings, you need not look too far to find reports where the process has gone very wrong; with superintendents being terminated or "resigning" in the infancy of their contracts for a multitude of reasons.

These actions leave communities polarized around what performance metrics drove these school district leaders out. The frequency of these stories highlight why thinking about the superintendent's evaluation process as a practicing superintendent and school board member is critical to both the short- and long-term success of district goals.

Salley's 1980 study examining the job functions of school superintendents contends that despite the varying demographics, size, and corresponding needs of a school district, the duties of a district leader remain largely the same. He posits that the prioritization of time and attention to multiple leadership responsibilities is what varies between districts. Consequently, Salley (1980) finds that there are wide differences in the methods used to evaluate district leaders and he further argues for a need to have clear understandings of what is to be evaluated and discerning procedures that lead to evaluation systems. Moreover, he contends these systems should be tied to district priorities and not situational outcomes or the prerogatives of select board members.

The elements needed to ensure an effective performance appraisal for the superintendent should encompass policy language, a relevant job description, and a shared understanding of the instrument to be utilized to conduct the evaluation, as the evaluation is a key component of the board–superintendent relationship (Glaub 1983). A solid evaluation process will help the board better discern its own efficacy as well as improve the superintendent's job performance.

This performance review should therefore be aligned with the accomplishment of annual goals that meet the board's expectations within a given school year (Glaub 1983). Evaluations are both about past issues and future interactions, and they have the potential to forge a narrative for how the relational dynamics between the board and the superintendent will play out in the years ahead (Glaub 1983).

The official establishment of the relationship between boards and superintendents is typically legitimized by documents written by individuals that are not actually working in schools. Contracts, job descriptions, and evaluation rubrics, along with board policies and administration manuals, all help to provide the skeletal outlines of how a relationship could proceed if it were truly representative of the "life" of a superintendent. However, while these documents exist, they are not often referenced unless something goes wrong, or there is a more immediate and pressing question that needs to be examined.

The information represented in these legal agreements creates a public record of topics relevant to school boards in considering the success of their superintendent. These documents tend to delineate terms and phrases for superintendent evaluation, such as the following:

- Success with regard to mutually agreed upon performance criteria
- General performance of the superintendent
- Working relationship between the superintendent and the board of education
- Progress toward completing individual goals
- Achievement of school district goals
- Execution of work compared to school district superintendent job description
- Performance when measured against performance-based criteria

- Overall conduct of the superintendent and growth in areas identified for improvement

These expressions are broad in their scope, general in their language, and allow for both personal interpretation and anecdotal evidence to suffice as standard measurements of performance. The challenges involved in leading the evaluation process this way is reflective of the shifting ground upon which public education is built. Change is a constant part of the current public education landscape; nonetheless, it is notably absent from the superintendent's performance criteria found in appraisal methodologies and procedural documents.

More succinctly stated, embedded in the daily life of a superintendent is a focus on leading and executing organizational change. However, the inevitable management of change required by this era of public education reform has not yet become consistent in the language utilized to evaluate superintendents. Portis and Garcia (2007) find that change is not only ever present in superintendent leadership but is fraught with nuances related to the board–superintendent dynamic:

> Two fundamental challenges superintendents face as change leaders are overcoming resistance to reform and modifying the district's culture. Many superintendents conceded they didn't anticipate the massive effort required to transform the mental models of district personnel and board members so that they could see the district as a system, [and] understand their roles and responsibilities in a new light and increase their expectations of results. (Portis and Garcia, para. 24)

Combing through the aforementioned evaluatory phases, it is evident that the superintendent's relationship with the board remains the driving factor behind the evaluation. This description is shaped by the overall quality of theory supporting the evaluation of the superintendent. Hence, effectively building the board–superintendent relationship with regard to evaluation is something that takes deliberate and informed practice.

The idea of mutual collaboration and transparency between the board of education and its superintendent in developing and understanding performance criteria is a strong theme in the literature (Mayo and McCartney 2004; Fowler 1977; Calzi and Heller 1989). This preparation ensures a coherent entrance into the evaluative process and helps foster a dialogue about how progress will be measured.

Moving a relationship from a nondescript document to actual interactions among individuals demands effective planning and purposeful reflection about situations that may arise. All of these steps must be navigated through the board–superintendent relationship by embedding checkpoints in the formal evaluation process. These checkpoints should be clearly delineated as a mutually agreed upon reference.

Below is an abbreviated listing of topics confronted by school superintendents, each of which could lead to anecdotal judgments being made regarding superintendent performance by board members: athletics, technology, school safety, negotiations and contract settlements, academic achievement, standardized testing, communications, facilities, budget development and spending priority identification, employee benefits, public performances (concerts, plays, and other events), school closings, wellness and food service, busing, tax levies, graduation rates, and day-to-day district operations.

Each of the aforementioned areas are ripe for controversy. How one leader traverses through the decision-making process might vary greatly from how another superintendent navigates the same relative issues. Consequently, the contests of reaching decision points reside in the arena of relationships and communication. Some board members have described the amount of information they are asked to consider as the equivalent of "drinking from a fire hose," while others have expressed a desire that communication flow down to them like a waterfall, and up from the superintendent like a spring in the ground.

The task in developing communication expectations is to consider the following questions:

1. What mechanisms will be utilized to effectively communicate with your school board?
2. What are the protocols you wish to have in place to ensure that communication is flowing both from them to you and vice versa?
3. How do you manage expectations around communication?
4. What does your relationship with the board need to look like for you to be successful?

A number of districts have boards that perpetually operate at an altitude that obscures the day-to day functions of the district and this approach to governance may be working well for them. However, at times a superintendent needs the board to land a little closer to more critical issues to ensure that board trustees are among key communicators of active initiatives including relative policy development. Determining the board's level of engagement in district operations is dependent on the understandings about the particular roles of governance and management established by the board–superintendent relationship.

Sometimes board members operate outside of their respective roles, often referenced by superintendents as "micromanaging." This can be a circumstantial and sensitive subject for some boards. Nevertheless it is a significant component of reflective boardsmanship to ensure a consistent focus on policy and governance. The superintendent should also consistently review whether the board is operating as a governance team. For example, what is the board's mind-set when they demand that the superintendent fire a particular coach or decide to have a pre-meeting with union leaders before formal negotiations begin? Thus, figuring out the level at which your board is operating can be an essential first step toward building a meaningful relationship.

The board–superintendent relationship builds toward understanding the present challenges in running a contemporary school district, works to identify and preserve strategic priorities, and rests on results. More broadly, the relationship seeks to bring meaningful definition to the work and success momentum toward meeting the targeted outcomes of the district. Success momentum is marked by the internal motivation that flows from organizational leadership. This energy is naturally transferred in ways that enlist the generative thinking of collaborators that help organize actionable plans.

In terms of the continuum of the board–superintendent relationship, how does a school superintendent operationalize the promotion of a respectful and mutually beneficial partnership? An easy and straightforward on-boarding approach may be the best strategy.

Upon entry into a new school district, it is incumbent upon the new superintendent to promote an opportunity for a one-to-one meeting where each board member has a chance to discuss the following questions:

1. Why did you run for the board?
2. What part of the community provided the most support to your candidacy? Why?
3. What do you feel is the biggest challenge facing the school district?
4. What was the most difficult decision you have ever had to make as a board member?
5. What are your expectations regarding communication?

Each one of these conversations plays a role in constructing a framework for a larger conversation at a board work session regarding the board–superintendent norms. The importance of convening a board retreat within the first three to four months of any superintendency cannot be understated. Understanding the level of influence of each trustee, who they represent, and what they expect helps to inform not only professional practice but also provides the superintendent with context regarding the board's philosophical perspective of their evaluation. These individual discussions will also serve to enlighten the incoming superintendent about the level of board operations and their collective beliefs around communication. On the whole, the illumination of these shared expectations reflects how a board has operationalized its functions. Moreover, the orientation of the school board to focus on policy and governance versus day-to-day operations is a critical understanding that must not be overlooked when considering the schema in which the evaluation of the superintendent will be devised.

In the document, "Guidelines for Evaluating the Superintendent," Lewis (1975) posits that the evaluation of the school district superintendent outlines the shared responsibilities of both the board and the district leader. He finds best practice indicated that what is to be evaluated should be known well in advance of the evaluation taking place, and that the topical areas for evaluatory review and feedback be informed by the superintendent to present a more balanced evaluatory tool for all parties to the evaluation. Consequently, the purpose of the superintendent's evaluation can overtly be rooted in the need for the board to examine itself, justify its decision-making processes to multiple constituencies, and build a systematic process by which it can engage the superintendent in a conversation about job performance (Dittloff 1982; Kowalski 1998; First 1990).

A superintendent's evaluation is best executed when there is clear evaluatory criteria set by the local school board that is capable of being assessed through the chosen performance review methodology, and when the results of the evaluation are shared between the superintendent and the school board. This generates a mutual understanding regarding where the parties stand with one another (Calzi and Heller 1989). Mutual understandings emerge from a dialogue. This discourse should be ongoing and framed by executed documents, clear communication protocols, and established board–superintendent norms.

Given that the performance attributes and criteria of the superintendent evaluation are not as critical to the evaluatory process as the thinking that undergirds the process, a foundational philosophy for what the board wishes to accomplish as a result of the evaluation of the superintendent may come into view as a broad overarching statement of purpose (Calzi and Heller 1989). Accordingly, the philosophy supporting the evaluation may grow from the priorities and employment job description devised by a board of education (Calzi and Heller 1989).

Nonetheless, the following is a fair question for a superintendent to ask "What is the philosophy of the board with regard to my evaluation?" The board collectively should also consider a question prior to the evaluation process commencing: What are they attempting to communicate in this annualized ritual and do they know what it is?

If custom and tradition become the dominant factors in the process and the voices in the room do not equitably participate, how will this affect the outcome? Documenting the philosophical underpinnings of the evaluation and having them articulated upfront takes courageous leadership and can be the impetus for the board to think both collectively and individually about what it is they ultimately expect from the process and from the district's leader.

A good evaluation process will afford both parties an opportunity to clarify roles, measure progress, set time-bound goals, and check in on the status of the relationship between the board and the superintendent: holding that the philosophy behind the purpose of the evaluation may largely be developed around the board–superintendent relationship (Fowler 1977).

Another critical impetus for the evaluation of the superintendent is that it should inspire the school board to reflect upon its goals for the school system and how effectively the superintendent is working toward the completion of these expected outcomes (Dittloff 1982). Dittloff (1982, p. 41) notes the importance of the philosophy behind the evaluation stating, "the process your school system might develop for evaluating the superintendent, is not nearly as important as the philosophical approach you use in conducting the evaluation." Hence, an additional philosophical element that may set a foundation for the evaluation of the superintendent is board goal setting, articulation of measures for accomplishment, and the relationship that drives that conversation (Dittloff 1982).

The viewpoint regarding the purpose of superintendent evaluation differs across school districts and among school boards. A solid evaluation process affords boards an opportunity to reflect on their own progress, engage their superintendent regarding his or her performance, and anchor how future employment negotiations and decisions manifest within the framework of board–superintendent relations (Braddom 1986). In fact, the superintendent's contractual agreement is among the only avenue that the board has to incentivize and reward high-level performance. In contrast, boards send messages about their dissatisfaction with the superintendent's performance in both relational and contractual dimensions.

A deliberative evaluation philosophy is naturally entrenched in two concurrent ideals. This first is that the evaluation process should help the superintendents improve their performance. Second, the appraisal methodology should foster open and honest communication between the board and its sole district employee. A review of board practice reveals that a small percentage of school boards utilize the evaluatory process to help the superintendent reflect on his or her job actions and suggest ways that they may improve in regard to job performance (Bippus 1985).

The evaluative process may provide an opportunity for school boards to present their concerns to their superintendent and foster a constructive dialogue before a situation becomes unsustainable, or worse yet, irreparable. It can also be a vehicle that empowers the superintendent to share with the board how he or she perceives the concerns and challenges raised as a result of the evaluatory methodology and criteria selected (Kibby 1965).

Eliciting conversations about how an individual is performing and the board's rate of success in directing its employee to meet district performance outcomes is an undertaking eschewed by some school boards. These conversations can be endemic with political pitfalls, particularly when the evaluation leans toward the subjective as opposed to more measurable objectives. As school board member elections can often change the makeup of the board, shifting the group dynamics at play in the evaluative process, Ornstein (1990) cautions superintendents about the ways the electoral process can upend superintendencies. He argues that superintendents must manage the confluence of needs and attributes that a school community develops in order to define a successful superintendency.

Schein (1996, p. 234) similarly notes that "cultures arise in whole occupational communities and that, therefore, parts of organizations are as much a reflection of the occupational backgrounds and experiences of some of their members as they are of their own unique organizational histories."

Thus, when a board changes its composition, the culture of the board can shift thereby furthering the need for ongoing conversation regarding the evaluation process and the ultimate goals and trajectory of a school district.

However, if the philosophy is clearly known, articulated, and agreed to by all parties, the seats that may flip over the course of a superintendency should not be able to immediately overturn agreed upon covenants between the board and the superintendent. Understanding how the board is comprised, coupled with the communication expectations and the nature of the board–superintendent relationship infuse the evaluatory philosophy and crystallize an organizing premise to the work.

When considering the framework for evaluation like a pyramid, the operating pattern is delineated in figure 1.1. Without a clear understanding from where the board is operating and its philosophical approach to the evaluation, it is likely to appear like a senseless quilt of fragmented information all sewn together for the sole purpose of meeting a contractual mandate. This is the equivalent of the proverbial square peg in a round hole. Instead, a concerted effort should be made to create a normed approach that guides the superintendent in their pursuit of meeting organizational needs and aspirations.

Historically, school boards provided many reasons as to why they did not conduct an evaluation of the district leader including difficulty in maintain-

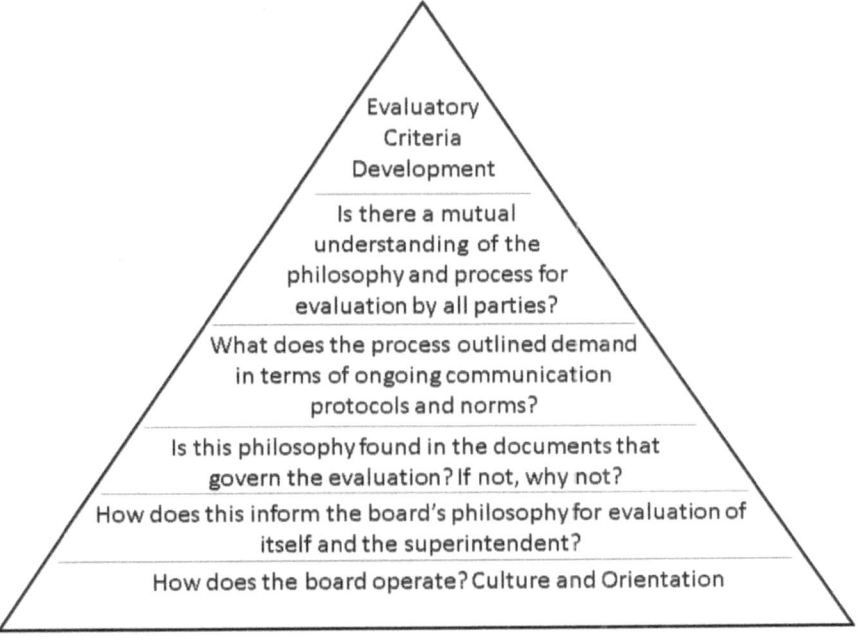

Figure 1.1. Foundational aspects supporting superintendent evaluation.

ing objectivity, ensuring that conflicting value judgments within a local school community do not consume the process, and the all-encompassing nature of the superintendency itself, thereby making it difficult to effectively evaluate (McCarty 1971).

Clear goals, aligned indicators, and outcomes that are mutually agreed upon and then measured afford a process that is more easily managed when considering the variables that could otherwise cloud the evaluation (McCarty 1971). Thus, abjuring the philosophical approach and arguing for a more objective one, McCarty (1971) maintains that the evaluation process be driven by an intentional course of action.

The rationale for conducting an evaluation of a school superintendent ranges from an objective-based approach with performance measured against individual goal completion, thereby limiting political machinations, to school boards utilizing the process to develop clear goals for the district. Yet, other board–superintendent partnerships utilize the process to assess internal school board dynamics, provide authentic feedback to the superintendent regarding job performance, appraise the school board–superintendent relationship, and survey the work of the district with regard to accomplishments and areas still in need of focus (Mayo and McCartney 2004).

The evaluation process that school districts utilize to assess the professional efficacy of the school superintendent most often falls along a continuum ranging from a checklist to a narrative format (Powers 2017; Castallo 1999; Booth and Glaub 1978). Within this array of choices, there is opportunity for politics, personal agendas, and superficiality to dominate the documentation of the superintendent's performance (Mayo and McCartney 2004). Castallo (1999) found that a rubric-based approach that sets out clear standards for performance related to critical topics regarding the superintendent's job performance has the most value in informing the process by which a superintendent is evaluated. However, Castallo (1999) also found that boards rarely take the time to develop such a systematic methodology when it comes to evaluating the superintendent.

Consider that school boards are made up of volunteers that have a multitude of tasks in their daily lives. They manage families, jobs, and sometimes schooling of their own. They have aging parents and young children. They occasionally find themselves having to travel for work or volunteering on multiple community boards. Board members are busy people.

Further, they have to manage their commitments to the board, read informational updates, attend meetings and subcommittee meetings, maintain visibility at events and community gatherings, and be a force for the initiatives they wish to champion at the board table. Hitting the pause button on all of this activity to stop and think about the superintendent's evaluation outside of the time period set forth by the contract is a challenging venture.

Managed thoughtfully, the superintendent's appraisal process demands a comprehensive communication strategy to successfully produce a solid framework for evaluation. Martin and Martin (1992) described the process of school board–superintendent communication to be limited by the lack of understanding school district leadership has about the board they work for:

> Unfortunately, many communications board members receive are ineffective simply because those who send them know very little about the personal or demographic characteristics of those receiving the message. . . . Effective communication must not only be relevant and reliable; it must also take into account the personal and demographic characteristics of the target population. Ignoring the age, sex, education level, and occupational background of school board members may be less likely to produce better informed board members than it is to produce just plain bored members. (Martin and Martin 1992, p. 420)

For this communication gap to be closed, leadership and patience is required and the nature of the relationship between the board and the superintendent becomes even more essential. Without this investment, the process is robbed of its potential to advance the district and inform professional practice. Dedicated time is a key commodity of the work in devising an evaluation protocol.

Dickinson (1980) outlines that a school board must invest the time to devise a thoughtful evaluation procedure. A school board must make a systematic effort to identify the legal obligations of the superintendent, define the scope of responsibility of the superintendent, evaluate the degree to which the superintendent actually can control those domains, and then build a criteria-based evaluation system that allows for authentic feedback. All of these elements must be grounded in a formalized timetable in which the board and the superintendent agree regarding how the evaluation process will proceed over the course of a given school year (Dickinson 1980).

While there is not a normative approach to evaluating a superintendent, it is imperative that there is transparency regarding the purpose for the evaluation, the evaluative tool to be used, and the evidence to be collected that exists on both sides of the table (Roelle and Monks 1978). It is incumbent upon the superintendent to take time to orient new board members to the evaluation process and document efforts toward goal completion in board meeting minutes to create a running record of what has been accomplished during the year (Roelle and Monks 1978).

Roelle and Monks (1978) concurred with the findings of Boyd (1966) that there is no one standardized way for a board to evaluate a superintendent. Additionally, boards must be mindful about the ability of a superintendent to effectively carry out board goals within the constraints imposed by the financial, political, and staffing limitations of a school district.

Beyond the workaday topics that define a superintendent's job, it is also important for school boards to consider the managerial style of the district's leader (Akenhead 1984). This suggests that districts assess both the work and style of the superintendent to capture an accurate appraisal of how he or she was perceived within the parameters of the relationship developed with the board of education (Akenhead 1984). Additionally, Akenhead (1984) stated that the conversations that flow from the analysis of management styles enable a more robust discussion about how a superintendent can better align his or her work with the interests and needs of the school board.

Booth and Glaub (1978, p. 26) state unequivocally that "the most important part of appraisal is to determine precisely what it is that you wish to appraise." They posit that all parties must approach the evaluation with the same understanding of what is to be measured and how that analysis will take place. They further state that the process must be aligned to the needs of the school district, refrain from subjective rating summaries and checklists, and that there be inherently meaningful opportunities for the school board and the superintendent to build a relationship.

Booth and Glaub (1978, p. 39) outline that in order for any appraisal process to have a chance of truly fostering a productive dialogue, the superintendent and the school board spend time with the following:

1. Getting to know one another
2. Eliminating minor differences of opinion and petty gripes
3. Defining the respective roles and responsibilities
4. Identifying strengths and weaknesses in both behavior and performance (results)
5. Planning improvements
6. Analyzing results of improvement plans

Booth and Glaub (1978) argue that the condition of the relationship between the board and the superintendent supports any effective evaluatory procedure. Verbiage that leads to best practice in building this relationship should exist in policy or as an extension thereof and be revisited as situational dynamics can change within a district.

Banks and Maloney (2007) found in a study of school district superintendents and school board presidents in the State of Washington that the human dimensional aspects that are interwoven within the evaluation procedure development can at times be overlooked or underdeveloped because of the fear that exists in disturbing the board–superintendent relationship. Board members are not typically trained evaluators of leadership performance. Diving head first into the evaluation of the superintendent without engaging in the requisite groundwork will appear daunting and create barriers to developing concepts that both parties hope to see included in the process.

As districts prioritize their individualized needs, boards have constructed a multitude of methodologies to assess the efficacy of their superintendent. Oftentimes, the evaluation process of the school superintendent is outlined by legal mandates tied to accountability standards both at the state and local levels. This approach fails to consider the varying characteristics of superintendents based on their managerial styles and training.

Boards looking to provide an evidentiary basis for their support of the superintendent prioritize installing a formal evaluation process. This convention must be partnered with a review of their philosophical approach and relative methodologies for expected outcomes of the process. When this criteria is absent, the superintendent's job performance is at times tied to evaluatory characteristics that are more politically expedient than embedded in instructional outcomes for students. This scenario can result in a more relationally based evaluation than one that is driven by an analysis of actual performance.

How districts evaluate the efficacy of school district leadership is premised upon how the stakeholders view the process and interact with a range of considerations. Laws requiring evaluation, promulgated standards, and contractual methodologies all contribute to how a district measures the success of its leader. Nonetheless, however, the evaluation boils down to a tenuous balance of how school boards interpret the superintendent's job description, their own policies, and the published goals of the district (Jones 1981).

From these documents, four essential domains emerge from which boards instigate the evaluation of the school superintendent. These domains consist of personal characteristics, administrative style, general management skills, and professional knowledge (Jones 1981).

Within these respective areas, local boards undertake the evaluation of a superintendent using multiple approaches including checklists, the employment of a narrative, or a more objective-based methodology (Jones 1981). Consequently, the evaluative process of a superintendent's performance review is most often a permutation of the four domains and the three styles of evaluation documents.

The framework for evaluating a superintendent's performance is often a blended process consisting of both formal and informal components (Carol 1972). While the typical evaluation characteristically results in boards rendering a decision premised upon superintendents' achievement of goals, inherent practices also entail superintendents' reflections on their job performance or a more self-directed reflection that the board uses as the evaluatory document (Carol 1972).

The criteria of curriculum development, stakeholder relations, general knowledge of education, educational leadership, longitudinal planning, district management, budget development and implementation, and personal qualities are all topics commonplace in the evaluation of a school district leader that inform the processes selected by individual school districts (Carol 1972).

Booth and Glaub (1978) devised a series of steps that boards and school district leaders can utilize to effectively develop a performance appraisal system to meet their ubiquitous needs. This system is designed around a construct that asks school boards to consider why they wish to evaluate the superintendent, synthesize the criteria they aspire to evaluate, clearly define the process the board will utilize in rendering an appraisal on performance, and to purposely deliberate on what they hope to achieve as a result of undergoing the process of evaluating the job performance of the district leader (Booth and Glaub 1978).

Two critical issues that boards must consider are the "factors the board as a whole considers important in measuring a superintendent's effectiveness" and "whether evaluation should be based on performance (results) or behavior (methods used) or some other criteria" (Booth and Glaub 1978, p. 13).

The answers to these questions may direct the evaluation process; however, questions remain as to how often they are efficaciously asked. Carol

(1972) found that superintendent evaluations are often organized around historic practices in a district, based upon agreements with previous superintendents, and often not revised in a timely manner by board members. Again, this is a symptom and by-product of the dearth in training that boards receive regarding the evaluation of the district's chief executive officer.

Devising specific and compelling goals that advance the superintendent's evaluation process requires a unified commitment from board trustees to objectively clarify the resultant performance outcomes (Fitzwater 1973). Fitzwater (1973, p. 26) contends that boards must make a concerted effort to move from the viewpoint of "our board evaluates the superintendent at every meeting, right out in public" toward clear objectives defined by effective actions that are capable of being measured.

The virtue of the selected model begins with the contractual relationship that the superintendent enters with the board of education. Kowalski (1998) asserts that the contract plays a critical role in outlining the responsibilities of the parties regarding evaluation and also plays an important part in curtailing the ability of politics and board factions from resetting a process midway through an evaluatory cycle. The contract, Kowalski (1998) holds, has the potential for spelling out the evaluatory instrument, the degree to which the job description of the superintendent will inform the evaluation, and the timeline and process for generating the evaluation.

In Mayo and McCartney's (2004) study of 1,125 school superintendents in the United States, utilizing a survey premised upon the work of Robinson and Bickers (1990), they find that the employment contract, while a source for criteria used in evaluation, has the potential to indistinctly define the evaluatory criteria. Moreover, they stress that the job description is only an effective tool for school boards if they have taken the time to update the description on a routine basis. Their study examines both the effectiveness of the evaluation process and how results-based performance metrics informed the evaluation of the school superintendent.

Mayo and McCartney (2004, p. 23) note that a uniformly effective results-based model for evaluating the superintendent of schools has yet to be developed stating, "an effective evaluation approach does not exist across the nation. Notwithstanding, results-based practices are nearly nonexistent. The findings of this study show little evidence that evaluation processes have changed to accommodate the 'accountability movement'"; these systems remain mired in traditional performance review practices.

Thus, while the job description, employment agreement, and policies regarding evaluation constitute the objective touch-points of subjective processes, some boards have worked to find ways to expand upon the evaluatory process moving the evaluation process away from the superintendent toward the annual evaluation of the district as a whole (Banks and Maloney 2007). This shifts the major focus to broader questions aligned to organizational goals: "Has the district [superintendent] operated within the bounds of acceptable behavior for how those results are to be achieved as described by the community [board]?" (Banks and Maloney 2007, pp. 10–11).

This movement toward district goals as opposed to individual performance objectives also places the role of the school district leader in a more instructionally centered position. Pajak and Glickman (1989, p. 64) found that if districts are to improve, "what is important is to create district expectations of professional dialogue and support so that educators in all positions in a school system can share in that inventiveness and express that commitment." The methodology of measuring superintendent effectiveness such as the one described above, however, is far more the exception than the rule.

This shift toward measuring instructional leadership, if it is occurring, is a relatively new phenomenon. In a 1985 survey of approximately seven hundred school superintendents in New York State, researchers found that board and community relations and fiscal management—along with general administration of the district, curriculum development, professional development, and human resources—all ranked higher in evaluatory criterion than student academic performance and achievement regarding data used to generate a superintendent's evaluation (Ehrenberg, Chaykowski, and Ehrenberg 1988). The researchers also noted the scarcity of objective measurements to assess each of these areas and the challenges this presents in evaluating a superintendent's job performance without prejudice (Ehrenberg, Chaykowski, and Ehrenberg 1988).

The impetus to evaluate a superintendent effectively must also overcome the lack of desire many school boards have to measure a superintendent's leadership ability. Though their published ideas span seventeen years, Banks and Maloney (2007) and First (1990) describe the fear and disquieting nature evaluations can bring to a superintendent and school board. First (1990) notes that this is particularly true because the depth and breadth of the superintendent's daily job responsibilities often make it hard to discern objective ways of measuring the success of the superintendent by board members.

Superintendents have often noted that there is a gap in understanding by boards about the arduous nature of system change and what leadership skills are actually required for successful district transformation. The explanation for this is a simple math equation. Superintendents are leading the district around the clock and have intel from primary data and persons within the district. To the contrary, board members are governing at public meetings, during limited subcommittee work, and accessing information that is further away from verifiable sources.

Regarding superintendent evaluations, Hawkins (1972, p. 42) states, "for the most part we have attempted to evaluate traits that are not only subject to a great deal of subjectivity and interpretation, but many of the things we have evaluated may have a low priority in the scheme of things." Ultimately, there are elements of politics that invade the evaluatory experience of the superintendent (Hoyle and Skrla 1999).

The political nature of what represents a pressing concern at the time of the evaluation often challenges the construct of what gets measured in an evaluation (Hoyle and Skrla 1999). This can include such items as not attending a parent–teacher association (PTA) meeting of a school favored by a particular board member or a regional dinner highlighting the accomplishments of non-district trustees. Navigating this political hotbed is a precarious component of the relationship forged between the board of education and the superintendent and should be grounded in discussion marked with candor and mutual respect.

A common element evaluated within the superintendent's appraisal is the board–superintendent relationship. This relationship is often loosely outlined in job descriptions, contracts, and established performance metrics; however, it must be enhanced by leadership skills, collective understandings, and the ability of a school board to appreciate the many dimensions that comprise school district leadership.

> Volumes have been written about this relationship, but how the board fulfills its role in evaluating superintendent performance may do more to define the board's opportunity for success in this relationship than any other one board activity. (Horn 1996, p. 20)

A particular component that adds to the trials of the relationship is the challenge of divergent understandings of the educational system between board members and superintendents. Kalkhoven (1981) writes

> By and large, school board members are lay citizens, not trained in the art of evaluation, particularly not evaluation of professional educators. This can become a very intimidating task when one compares his or her own educational credentials with the superintendent's. (Kalkhoven 1981, p. 6)

This attribute has at least, in part, been recognized by some states that have called for stronger board governance training regarding superintendent and board evaluation. However, research exists as to how general principles of leadership can inform evaluation practices at the school district level.

Alternatively, and equally important, is the superintendent's consistent awareness of this kind of volunteer community activism. Community members seek these roles for a milieu of reasons that run the gamut of being emphatically happy with the education their children received thereby inciting a wish to "pay it forward" or because they are vehemently dissatisfied with the education system and/or its leadership. Despite the inherent motivation of board trustees, a superintendent should leverage their ability to center the direction of the district and board on shared goals. The superintendent must also possess the temperament and ability to put aside their ego for the sake of consistently elevating board–superintendent discussions to focus on the greater good.

Stronge (1998) believes that there is a case to be made between leadership in schools and business organizations with regard to the skills necessary to be an effective leader. Further, Richardson, Lane, and Flanigan (1996, p. 291) find in their study of characteristics of successful principals that teachers and business leaders identify the attributes of being "honest, competent, forward-looking and inspiring" as most desirable in both education and business leadership. Hence, applying general leadership understandings to the superintendent evaluation process can support board members in transferring their experiences in their professional domains to their responsibilities in evaluating the district leader.

The nature of the superintendent–board relationship comes down to the degree of candidness each side expects of the other (Fowler 1977). If the parties are willing to engage one another in the maintenance of open communication and develop opportunities to collaboratively problem solve, the relationship often leads to a meaningful evaluatory process (Fowler 1977; Chand 1984).

When boards operate the evaluative process toward their own objectives in a more clandestine fashion and cultivate a sense of distrust among the parties, that culture fosters "hidden agendas" and can breed secrecy on the part of the superintendent regarding their job performance (Foldesy 1989). To some degree, the nature of this relationship is initiated well before the contract negotiations begin and is forged as part of the hiring process when the board establishes the criteria for superintendent candidates (Clear 1983).

"The effectiveness of evaluation depends, not upon a particular plan or format, but rather upon the degree of mutual interest which exists between the board and superintendent" (Lindgren 1985, p. 16). This "mutual interest" is fostered when a clear effort is made to collaboratively set goals and benchmarks to be included as part of the evaluative process (Eadie 2003). Swain (1975) contends,

> First goals and objectives must be established, along with the methods and criteria for evaluating whether or not the goals and objectives have been attained. Then they must be written, either into policy or the administrator's contract. (Swain 1975, p. 5)

The elements of candidness, the lack of hidden agendas, and the fostering of a mutual interest in the evaluative process speak to what Eadie (2003) holds when he argues the following:

> At the heart of every truly high-impact school board is a solid board–superintendent working partnership, and one of the most effective ways to keep that partnership healthy and productive is a well-designed process for board evaluation of the superintendent. (Eadie 2003, p. 29)

However, Mitchell (1994, p. 32) found that superintendents perceive "school boards change the rules on them all the time. They think they are tackling the major problems in their districts; then they find out the boards had different priorities." Balancing this conflated dynamic sometimes found within a board–superintendent relationship often becomes a critical component of establishing and maintaining the relative criteria of the evaluatory process (Jones 1994).

The development of an effective evaluation process is not intuitive to the board–superintendent relationship (Abrams 1987). Abrams (1987) argues that the impetus to advocate for an objective evaluation falls to the superintendent and is only achieved when the assessment instrument is collaboratively developed with the board and evaluatory criteria has fidelity to a given job description. The individualization of the evaluatory process for the superintendent by each board plays an important role in ensuring that the evaluation is pertinent to the stakeholders of the evaluation (Chand 1984).

Failure to personalize the evaluation process and evidentiary documents may leave the superintendent feeling evaluated by criteria that is not applicable to them. Grady and Bryant (1991) find the following in their study of school board presidents and their superintendents' handling of critical situations facing their respective school districts:

> The most frequent cause of tension between a school board and its superintendent has nothing to do with administrivia or ethics and everything to do with human relations. Put simply, poor people skills are the common cause of tense times between superintendents and their boards. (Grady and Bryant 1991, p. 24)

Tallerico (1989, p. 218) finds that board members and their interactions with the superintendent fall along a continuum that ranges "from passive acquiescence to proactive supportiveness to resistive vigilance" and that these interactions were fostered by "the distinct ways in which information is collected and utilized, and the scope, purpose and degree of board member involvement in school district affairs."

How a district devises its governance structure, how individual board members perceive their role, how information is disseminated, and how board members and superintendents interact on the basis of their personal qualities all coalesce to build essential elements of the board–superintendent dynamic within a district (Tallerico 1989).

Consider how the relational dynamic can play out in a routine matter as simple as having a board member visit a school. Certainly, a board member may want to glean information relating to the operations of a school building; however, how they approach that process can have a true effect on the relationship and the degree of trust built between the board and the superintendent. Separating the personal dimensions from the governance practice coalesces into a genuine situation that a board and superintendent must be able to successfully navigate.

The board of education has set governance policy by which they conduct themselves. Within these guidelines, the full board has agreed that all trustees will alert the president and superintendent when visiting any school building within the district. One trustee, and former board president, has recently spent extended time in school buildings without alerting the current board president or the superintendent. The reasons for these visits have varied included interacting with district staff to gain information about ongoing construction projects or current searches for certificated employees.

The superintendent has a strong working relationship with this trustee and has been able to engage this member in conversations that result in reasonable reflection on the part of the board member. In turn, this trustee pledges that his future actions will align with agreed upon governance protocols. Soon after this promise of reforming his actions, this board member visits the central office and questions one of the assistant superintendents about a vendor that lost a long-time contract with the district.

After being alerted by her assistant about the board member's latest inquiry, the superintendent enlists the assistance of the board president and asks him to speak to his colleague about his failure to follow the compact between the board and superintendent. What she assumes will be a private conversation between the board president and his colleague erupts into an executive session to vehemently review the communication protocols from which the superintendent is excused.

In the next week, the superintendent notices that the relationship status of the aforementioned trustee has eroded to him barely making eye contact with her. The exchange between the two of them is strained, at best, and other members begin asking the superintendent if they have done anything that the superintendent might consider "overreaching" their authority.

The superintendent goes back to the board president to question him about what happened in executive session, and he comments that the trustee that failed to follow the communication protocols was out of control and had to be stopped. The board president further explained that he simply reviewed the governance protocols with the full board. By now, the superintendent realizes that what should have been a private gentle reminder for one board member has turned into a harassing accusation and affront to the full board. She will have to triple her efforts to repair the damage that was done to the trustful board–superintendent relationship that she had worked so hard to build before the clandestine executive session.

Indeed it is the shared understanding by board members and the superintendent of their respective roles in the governance process that contributes much to the parameters of the relationship (Hayden 1986). If the roles of the various parties to the evaluation are not clearly understood—and that feeds into the evaluative process—challenges can emerge that may undercut the efficacy of the board–superintendent relationship (Hayden 1986).

However, the clearer the organizational goals are defined by the board of education, and the more time spent working toward their completion, the more apt that the board–superintendent dynamic stays positive (Brodinski 1983).

The beginning of any superintendency requires the superintendent to take decisive action in setting up norms and protocols regarding the evaluation and the board–superintendent relationship. Putting in this effort up front builds a dynamic of shared understandings that enables the superintendent to confidently develop supports for the evaluation process and their ability to effectively complete the work ahead.

Think carefully about the pyramid in figure 1.1, and now on the y-axis add the elements of time to generate this process; training, to ensure board members have an understanding of how to approach the evaluation of the superintendent; relationship construction incorporating communication and understanding of who the board members are as individuals; and leadership (see figure 1.2).

The higher up you go on the pyramid, the more complex this work becomes. Given the task, the antidote often lies in the leadership practices of the superintendent requiring a focus on all aspects of building alliances within these working relationships. Necessarily, there are more informal approaches to building relationships with the board that manifest as unplanned visits by individual trustees or unexpected evening phone conversations.

It is during these times that the superintendent learns more about districtwide issues that have vexed the community and past boards, and that contin-

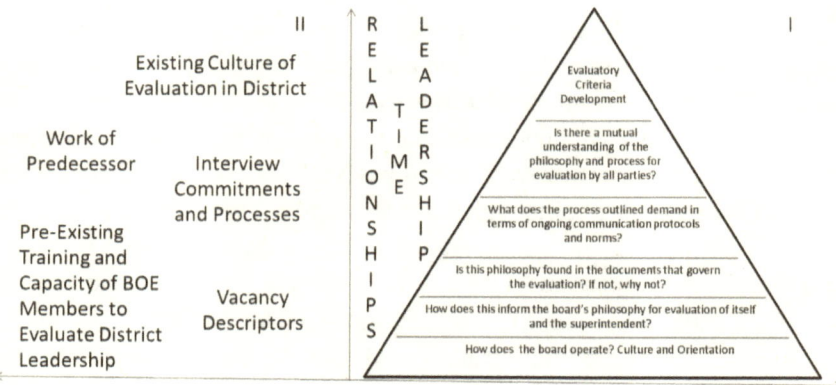

Figure 1.2.   Quadrant-two factors that influence evaluation.

ue to be active forces thwarting desired progress. These unresolved problems must be dealt with in ways that advance the board–superintendent relationship to minimize the withdrawal of energy that could be expended for more deliberate commitments.

Chapter Two

Institutional Memory

There is something to be said for the perpetual impact of institutional memory. The experiences, traits, and characteristics of an organization become the convergent backdrop to the value sets of school boards and their constituents. The storms a district weathered before the superintendent arrived, what they discovered about themselves during tribulations while waiting for a new superintendent(s) to appear, and why they think the next leader will be able to accomplish specific endeavors all forge an unspoken understanding about the district, its past, and its potential future. This vested impression often reveals itself in the way a board approaches a superintendent's evaluation and in how they construct the language that documents the evaluation in job descriptions, policies, and employment contracts.

The contract is a powerful tool to set the expectations for performance appraisal. The development of the contract is a time to establish language around setting goals, midyear conferencing, the evaluation process, and the purpose of the final product. The contract language relating to evaluation anticipates the mitigation of variables that seek, by natural force, to permeate the evaluation process.

Board capacity for evaluation, prior superintendent performance, and community expectations coalesce into considerations for not only the evaluation, but moreover how the employment contract speaks to the evaluation process. Hendricks (2013) finds the following:

> In order to maintain a successful relationship, it is imperative that a well-designed performance evaluation tool is implemented. Therefore, it is essential that formal guidelines are established because they can provide both guidance

and standards throughout the superintendent performance evaluation process. (Hendricks 2013, p. 64)

The employment contract is the initial starting point for the development of the guard rails to the lane-driven evaluation process. This idea supports the premise that philosophy trumps criteria, and that active evaluative procedures require mutual conversations that generate both trust and transparency. If the documents state one thing, but the language presents a conflicting rationale, the absence of an effective relationship and understanding of institutional memory can distort the more highly valued elements of leadership by a board of education. This is an extremely slippery slope that quickly dissolves into the old adage of "knowing too little too late."

Understanding how the predecessor was perceived by both the board and the community and what criteria was applied to the evaluation are valuable components toward finding the starting point for either conversation about—or wholesale departure from—past practice. If you accept the premise that many boards evaluate new leadership in the same fashion as they had the former superintendent, bending the paradigm toward the arc of transparency requires historical knowledge and cultural understanding.

As established, some boards do not formally evaluate their superintendent unless there is an imminent need. Others engage in a performance review that allows spurious praise in an effort to avoid conflict or that reflects the political schema of the district at a given point in time. Finally, there are boards that deliver legitimate feedback that grows the superintendent's authority and capacity to meet the global needs of the district.

While it is difficult to interpret what motivated the actions of the preceding organizational leader, how this work was received by the majority of the community can permeate a dominant role in organizational memory. More pointedly, the perception of past leadership efforts directly impacts how the incoming superintendent approaches the expectations about his or her service to the district.

In cases where prior leadership was well favored, identifying areas in need of improvement can be disquieting and runs the risk of alienating board members as they potentially hired the previous district leader and may have positively evaluated their progress. Therefore, the new superintendent must determine how to lift the conversation from the mire of personal feelings to a more intellectual journey about innovative ways to collaboratively face district challenges as an important step in the evaluation process.

Organizational perception or how a school district perceives itself is an equally important part of the evaluation narrative.

- If the school community and board share the view that their schools are successful predicated on test scores, but few students who graduate from the district survive the opening months of a college experience, are they successful?
- If a district rarely raises the tax levy, but by adopting this philosophy allows for the facilities to face mounting costs due to deferred maintenance, have they made the right decision?
- When a district highlights the academic achievement of its students while failing to bring forward the disaggregated trend data regarding student skill development, is it really engaged in what many public school mission statements purport about educating all children?

Acceptably high graduation rates coupled with a low tax levy, and publicity highlighting raised student achievement, may infuse the evaluation process with ideas of solid performance by prior leadership. This can increase the challenges of the incoming superintendent who may face the dual tasks of presenting organizational concerns and shifting individual board member positions to a more urgent mind-set about meeting the strategic actions that they otherwise may have little knowledge of at the board level. Broadly, this dissonance is festooned with pitfalls and demonstrates how the board–superintendent relationship along with a lack of transparency quickly converge well before a superintendent takes the district's helm.

Public school boards, particularly those that have long-standing members, have experiential histories that can confound a targeted approach to appraising the current superintendent's performance. There are times that lingering memories of a district's poor performance work to the advantage of the debuting superintendent; in other instances, musings about distorted high performance can cast a nostalgic shadow over the rising superintendent.

Ultimately, time and the confrontation of new questions about student success rates energize the dissipation of this convenient reverie. This process renews the inherent and cyclical nature of pairing board–superintendent relationships with institutional memory. It also activates the merger of the mutually exclusive talents of the full governing board toward the collective goal of resolving novel issues.

The group dynamics of the board of education and district culture can be sussed out in the interview process with a guided focus on the interview questions. It is not uncommon for boards to reveal the ideas and understandings of their district in the questions they ask superintendent candidates during the interview. For example, what priorities are communicated when board members make the following inquiries?

1. How will you deal with the teacher union's practice of wearing black shirts on Wednesday as a symbol of their displeasure with the rate of teacher pay?
2. How do you feel about the new state learning standards being tied to teacher evaluations?
3. Do you think that teacher salaries are adequate for this particular region?

Listening for topics that are not mentioned during these conversations can tell a candidate even more about the board of education's impression of what they wish the new superintendent to address and their beliefs about necessary strategic improvements. It is important to attend to the energy that surrounds a search and positive district attributes that are presented to attract a candidate equally. These highlights are routinely projected by specialized search firms and can blunt fact-driven challenges and expectations of new leadership.

The groundwork for a superintendent's success is being laid well before he or she applied for the position. The board, employees, and various community stakeholders are encouraged by search firms to create a schema of desirous characteristics in a new superintendent including their hopes about what the ideal candidate will accomplish. This value center must not be overlooked as it is directly linked to the design of the evaluation process. In other words, these aspirational feelings are inevitably factored into judgments submitted about the superintendent's leadership and relative achievements.

Acknowledging and understanding these superficial factors does not soften the stark and surprising reality that this thinking seeps into the development of evaluation processes and proposed outcomes. The best evaluation tools can be ill-fated unless the requirement of transparency and evidentiary-based evaluation protocols are embedded throughout the appraisal process. This is "the work before the work."

Boring (2011) finds that the profile description for a superintendent is predicated on three major areas:

> The conventional pattern in portraying the important elements for a superintendent position is to develop descriptions for at least three dimensions: The personal qualities or characteristics desired in the new superintendent; the qualifications felt important or desirable in a new superintendent; and the challenges of the job as the new person assumes responsibility to lead the school district. (Boring 2011, p. 13)

The early processes of superintendent selection are designed to foster a process that enables district stakeholders to

> Define a district's issues, determine the qualifications needed to address them, and design a strategy to identify and attract the best possible candidates. Tough organizational issues demand premium candidates. But far too often, school boards and candidates are constrained by flaws in traditional superintendent search methodologies. (Jernigan 1997, p. 8)

These "flaws" may be related to who has input into the hiring process, the degree to which confidentiality is maintained, and the willingness of those charged with conducting the search to screen the entire candidate pool in relation to the qualifications outlined in the job posting.

Tallerico (2000) finds that while these elements were developed as part of the search process

> The listings of near-generic competencies that appear in many superintendency vacancy advertisements (e.g., excellent communication skills, instructional leadership ability, knowledge of budgeting and finance), school board members' and consultants' behind-the-scenes definitions of candidate quality rely more on hierarchies of prior job titles than on particular leadership skills. (Tallerico 2000, p. 29)

Thus, it is the institutional memory, the backstory, that can reveal itself in the questions a board asks and the research a candidate conducts. It is within these actions that the successful candidate can potentially find the most accurate information about what tasks will need his or her immediate attention and direct oversight.

An informed perspective regarding the functions and purpose of a governing board has a significant impact on understanding the capacity of the role of the superintendent, particularly as it relates to change management.

Let us presume that school boards exist in a constant state of evaluation. The effectiveness of a particular program, the budgetary impact relative to the perceived programmatic value, and how the administration implements this initiative are all cause for a board to undergo some form of evaluation activity. These judgments may provoke minimal commentary or they can drive conversations over multiple interactions. In each instance, however, the evaluatory activity is being assessed against an internal set of values, unless the superintendent has disrupted this thinking by providing new evidentiary information.

In this way, the superintendent can successfully challenge institutional memory correcting particular feelings or discernment with sincerity and truthfulness. The traditional training board members have regarding boardsmanship, the evaluation of programs, and people are fairly limited. Hoyle and Skrla (1999) hold the following:

> Board training about the superintendent's evaluation should not be viewed as a luxury to be indulged in if time and money allow. It is unreasonable and unrealistic to expect board members to do a good job at something for which they have had no training, and in the case of new board members who are elected annually, no experience. (Hoyle and Skrla 1999, p. 417)

Most of the professional advice that board members receive about how to successfully conduct the superintendents' evaluation is produced by those organizations where boards provide financial support through membership dues. This is problematic in that the projected information is mostly generated and delivered by well-intentioned professionals that may be prejudiced by the implicit bias of maintaining the high membership levels that support the survival of their regional and state organizations. Moreover, for the most part, the individuals delivering this information have never been practicing superintendents. This is a missed opportunity to have a straightforward and candid discussion led by an experienced superintendent that has been on the alternate side of this process.

The assignment of a value judgment within the performance evaluation of the superintendent does not necessarily equate to the board's full understanding of the stated situation; nor does it mean that each individual engaged in the appraisal process has developed an authentic conception of the multiple layers of leadership required to effectively complete the necessary work. A case in point is as follows:

In a rural school district deep in the heart of dairy country, an elementary building allows students to purchase ice cream on Fridays from the school cafeteria. The students have enjoyed this tradition for many years and look forward to "ice cream Fridays" all week.

Nevertheless, each Friday there is a group of students whose parents cannot afford the ice cream and those students sit during lunch and watch their friends enjoy their ice cream treats. Over time, students have been known to cry as some are frankly too young to fully understand why they cannot have ice cream. These ice cream Fridays have taken their toll on school personnel as well. Every Friday, the staff has its heart broken trying to explain "why" to the students disenfranchised by this weekly event, and trying to somehow convince themselves that students will be "okay" as a result of this repeated experience.

As the next school year starts, with the support of the superintendent, the principal eliminates "ice cream Fridays" with little fanfare. Aware that student poverty is rising and the gap between the haves and the have-nots is growing, allowing one-third of the school to watch the other two-thirds eat ice cream is causing a disruption to the learning environment. The parents of the students who can afford ice cream have their checks returned with the explanation that ice cream is no longer available at the school.

One board member questions the superintendent and wants to know, as other parents have been asking, "What is going on with the ice cream at the elementary school?" Another board member has his check returned that he sent to school to buy ice cream, but does not say anything to the superintendent. A third board member is very confused about why a school district supported by dairy farmers is eliminating ice cream from the school cafeteria. Two other board members contacted the superintendent and after a conversation agree that the poverty gap is growing at too fast of a rate to parade the disparity between the haves and the have-nots in such a public way at school.

In this scenario, one board member is representing parent feedback, another is waiting and watching to see how the situation will play out. A third trustee is considering the elimination of ice cream from the political perspective of the impact on the local economy, and two others questioned the superintendent, but are willing to focus on the topic of student poverty and its influence on the school environment at large.

Each of these board members engaged in an evaluation of this particular building-level change, ranging from how the elimination of ice cream was communicated, the reasons for ending the practice, the optics to the broader school community, and their ability to see the resultant effects over time. While these board members actively questioned this management change, they were not asked to evaluate it against a rubric, nor was it considered along a continuum of educational leadership standards. If the board decides to include this situation in the superintendent's formal evaluation, what should the narrative provide as evidence for the individualistic conclusions they reached about the abolishment of ice cream Fridays?

This is just one of multiple situations that the board will potentially contemplate when they are confronted with completing the superintendent's evaluation. Active participation in the explanation of an event related to leadership performance—that should be analyzed against a set of standards, thereby requiring supportive evidence to reach a collective decision about performance—is not innate to anyone's daily existence. It is fair to conclude that engaging in the complexities of this process without the benefit of targeted and effective training on evaluation is an arduous task for some board members.

Furthermore, it is important to know that the experience a board member has with the evaluation process may also be informed by outside pressures such as family, neighbors, and friends. The duress a board member may be under to take actions that communicate a message of responsiveness to outside concerns also informs the appraisal process. This can cause board members to artificially utilize the evaluation tool(s) relying on subjective sources and false knowledge of various events and topics. Henrikson (2018) notes,

> If the superintendent continues to prove his or her performance based on subjective and often misaligned evidence provided only by the superintendent and documented within a framework, that is not a transformative change. If the school board uses a similar method of subjectively approving said evidence based on their opinions of performance during one or two meetings per year, that is not a transformative change either. (Henrikson 2018, p. 25)

The superintendent has an imperative upon herself to ensure that the work they are undertaking in leading a district is documented in a way that board members find accessible and contributes to the narrative about their work. Without evidence of the work undertaken to achieve goals and objectives, to document efforts that are in alignment with the board's philosophy for evaluation and to demonstrate competency in evaluative domains, the superintendent leaves himself exposed for board members to fill the gaps with their own sense of understanding about what has been done or not done to their satisfaction.

Training on the evaluation process, its philosophy, purpose, and intent, coupled with the ability of the board to step outside of its comfort zone and critically reflect on the district and its leadership takes courage, capacity, and time. Both parties meeting each other honestly, and over time constructing a relationship that has meaning and acknowledges where both sides are coming from, plays a key role in shaping the evaluation of the superintendent.

This is often contrary to the manner in which the superintendent's evaluation process unfolds. Matthews (2001) finds that the evaluation process

> is often very simple. Forms are filled out by each school board member and sometimes summarized by the board chair. The board then discusses the results with the superintendent once a year during an executive session. Goals for the new year are agreed upon, and everybody goes home. (Mathews 2001, para. 2)

The lack of intentionality found in these processes are anchored in the nondescript nature of superintendents' contract language relating to evaluations. Hoyle and Skrla (1999) recommend that superintendents insist that elements of the evaluation including "how often the evaluation should take place, what data or evidence should be produced for each evaluation session, from whom the data will be collected, and who will do the evaluation" all be included in the negotiated contract language (Hoyle and Skrla 1999, p. 415).

This level of detail is rare as contracts are not typically written by practitioners and are designed by lawyers to insulate parties from liability and shield them from future reasons to challenge an idea or phrase.

In a qualitative study of superintendent contract language in New York State, Powers (2017) finds the following rating categories as overriding themes and general descriptors contained in contract language relating to superintendent evaluations, as shown in table 2.1.

The language contained in these documents lacks specificity, is vast in its dimensions, and ultimately provides the end-user with only a skeletal framework for the development of the evaluation. This ambiguity presents both superintendents and school boards with challenges relative to devising and articulating an effective approach to the evaluation process. There is minimal opportunity to collaborate on the evaluation language of the employment agreement. Without a comprehensive understanding of the general topics

Table 2.1. Topical categories relating to the evaluation of the superintendent as noted in employment contracts

Category name	Examples of language by category
The superintendent's working relationship with board	"The board shall devote at least one portion of a meeting during the months of October and February to an evaluation in executive session of his performance and his working relationship with the board" (District #20).
Superintendent progress toward goals	"The parties shall meet annually at a mutually agreeable time . . . to evaluate the superintendent including previous goals" (District #31).
Areas for improvement	"The evaluation shall include recommendations as to areas of improvement in all instances where the board deems performance to be needing improvement" (District #7).
General job performance	"The board shall base its evaluation of the superintendent's performance and progress toward the goals and objectives established by the superintendent and the board as set forth above, as well as on the general performance of the superintendent in carrying out his/her required duties and responsibilities" (District #5).
Mutually established performance criteria	"The evaluation shall be based upon performance criteria mutually established by the board and the superintendent" (District #13).
The alignment of performance to position description	"This evaluation shall be reasonably related to the position description of the superintendent" (District #23).
Measurements against given performance based criteria	"This evaluation of the superintendent shall review the goals and objectives set previously and the superintendent's success in meeting the goals and objectives for that year" (District #19).
Achievement of required duties and responsibilities	"The board shall base its evaluation upon the superintendent's performance and progress . . . in carrying out his required duties and responsibilities" (District #11).
Overall conduct	"The superintendent shall be evaluated by the board based on his overall conduct and activities while acclimating to the district" (District #1).

listed in the description of the superintendent's evaluation, there cannot be a true sense of purpose and supervision regarding the outcome of the process.

Contract language that accurately defines the procedure guiding the development of the superintendent's performance goals must also verify the mutually agreed upon measurements and process between the board of education and the superintendent. This will provide the necessary clarity for the purpose of establishing the objective criteria and rating system. Ultimately, these are the tools that will promote the shared ability among the board and superintendent to articulate the goals the superintendent will pursue during the course of a respective school year. According to O'Hara (1994),

> The board must clearly communicate performance expectations to the superintendent. This will enable them to accurately determine whether the superintendent has lived up to those expectations. . . . Ideally, the employment contract will require frequent evaluations and provide that the procedure and criteria to be used will be agreed upon jointly by the parties. (O'Hara 1994, para. 25)

Further, Hoyle and Skrla (1999, p. 417) conclude that "the superintendent's evaluation is too crucial of an event to be left to chance or to be left free to drift in the currents of district politics." Thus, the need for having clear contractual language to govern the politics, capacity, and historical (i.e., institutional memory) practices contained in a board's dynamic is apparent.

Goal setting plays a key role in moving the language of the contract from theory to practice. Superintendents' goals are derived by one of three methodologies: the superintendent writes the goals and shares them with the board, or vice versa, or the development of the goals of the district's instructional leader is a collaborative endeavor—especially choosing the metrics for assessing achievement. The contract language supporting these various methodologies is found in verbiage expressly outlining each of the practices listed above. Board-developed goals are found in contract language that places the authority to assign superintendent goals at the discretion of the board:

> The Board, at its option, may devote at least a portion of one meeting in or about the month of March in each year of the Superintendent's employment by the District to the development of a list of goals for the District for the ensuing year. A written memorandum summarizing the goals that the Board articulated shall be provided to the Board by the Superintendent subsequent to such discussion and the Superintendent shall attempt to effectuate those goals [District #42]. (Powers 2017, p. 62)

An example of the contractual language in which the superintendent develops individual goals and provides them to the board of education is found in statements such as the following:

> On or before September 1 of each school year of this Agreement, the Superintendent shall provide to the Board a written statement of the annual goals and objectives which the Superintendent intends to concentrate on during the upcoming school year [District #38]. (Powers 2017, p. 62)

However, perhaps the most common language found in contract language speaks to the collaborative nature of the goal-setting process between the superintendent and the school board. This is often outlined in contract language that reads, "the board shall devote at least a portion of one meeting prior to September 1 of each school year of the Superintendent's employment by the District to the cooperative development of a list of District goals for the ensuing school year [District #27]" (Powers 2017, pp. 62–63).

It is this cooperative and collaborative process that helps to build an effective board–superintendent relationship (O'Hara 1994). Goals that are well articulated and scaffolded by a shared vision between the governance team and the superintendent are a powerful touchstone that builds a shared sense of direction and purpose. Having a board that agrees with the goals because they coauthored them with the district's leader promotes steadfast moments that can conquer political turmoil and scrutiny. Also, having a collective will to accomplish shared longitudinal plans limits the intrusion of scattered curiosities that can derail the collective plans of the board and the superintendent. Waters and Marzano (2006) find that

> It is not unusual that individual board members pursue their own interests and expectations for the districts that they are elected to serve. This finding suggests, however, that when individual board member interests and expectations distract from board-adopted achievement and instructional goals, they are not contributing to the district's success, but, in fact, may be working in opposition to that end. (Waters and Marzano 2006, p. 12)

Thus, having a common awareness of the board's commitments in conjunction with the superintendent becomes a powerful contractual attribute to halt distractions from the genuine work of the district. The collaborative sense of purpose engendered by shared goals brings the need for ongoing dialogue about performance not only on the goals themselves but the action steps taken to attain them.

One step that superintendents and boards should contractually outline is a midyear evaluation conference. This "checkpoint" can be utilized by board members to have a less formal conversation focused on sharing ideas about how the execution of goals is progressing and articulate concerns. It is also a time to provide constructive feedback and ask questions before the year has ended. This strategy thwarts a process more liken to an autopsy where there is no way to address or remedy an area identified as needing additional work or improvement.

Midyear conversations have the power of illuminating discrepancies in the perceptions of both the superintendent and members of the board about the strategies and progress toward achieving articulated goals. Without the benefit of this stopgap, the gamut of these differences can become one of the main culprits in derailing the final evaluation discussion. Lost opportunities to rectify misconceptions about actions intended to realize measurable objectives leave both sides of the evaluation process at odds rather than engagement in the more positive movement of realigning a collective focus.

Equally important is the perpetuation of a reflective philosophy by boards of education including their consideration of how their practices for evaluating the superintendent are being realized through their own actions, and whether set goals are still reasonable as the result of changes that may have occurred since the start of the evaluation cycle. The contractual requirement of a well-defined midyear discussion is also prescriptive in scaffolding the exchange of evidentiary data relative to advancing the success of meeting targeted outcomes. Communicating this information in segments serves to deepen the boards' understanding of the massive undertaking represented by organizational change and the superintendent's concomitant efforts in this march toward agreed-upon results.

Hallinger and Murphy's 1986 study regarding superintendents' instructional leadership found that "symbolic leadership and collaborative processes in and of themselves will provide inadequate mechanisms for achieving and maintaining the district mission" (Hallinger and Murphy 1986, p. 230). Accordingly, having specific evidentiary data aligned to targeted goals that are supported by thoughtful relationships brings this worthwhile contractual language to life.

Indeed, the practice of having a midyear evaluation to mitigate potential pitfalls and rebalance professional goals is not a novel concept in the evaluation of a school superintendent. Cuban (1977) notes,

> Once a year is not enough because formal, year-end evaluations (and their follow-up conferences to discuss results) place too much emotional weight on the employee. They too easily become a garbage can for dumping an entire year's unresolved issues, unanswered questions, and untouched peeves. At least two formal conferences each year should be held between the board and

superintendent. The rationale is that a school board can influence the executive's behavior before the end of the school year. (Cuban 1977, p. 6)

Consequently, building language into a contract that allows for a midyear evaluation also helps to sustain the philosophical underpinnings of the evaluation process. Such language ensures that the conversation is brought up in a consistent and formulaic manner. This gives the evaluation process a better chance to remain true to a more purposeful aim and not be derailed by topics that are not integrally germane to the results-driven agreements established by the superintendent and trustees of the board. An example of the type of machinations that can often drain what we define as success momentum is described here.

Imagine that the superintendent attends what she believes to be a high number of student extracurricular events and activities including concerts, plays, parent meetings, and sporting activities. Additionally, four out of five days school is in session, she is visiting students in classrooms, observing instructional practices that reflect recent programmatic shifts, and generally promoting more opportunities to be in good relationships with her staff.

At her final evaluation meeting, the board delivers the shocking news that the superintendent needs to increase her visibility and attend more athletic functions. Instead of waiting for the end of the year where this perception cannot be corrected in real time, a midyear conference is a more effective avenue to raise concerns, review relevant information, and devise an action plan to submit and address this issue.

The merits of the midyear conference can also be illustrated during the times of the year devoted to prioritizing budget items for an upcoming school year. Examine the following scenario.

It is not uncommon for superintendents to face mounting pressures to raise students' standardized reading and math scores. In this district, students have been falling behind in reading and the skill gap is widening and becoming more apparent at the upper grades. The superintendent has been diligently working on ensuring that all students are reading at a commensurate level by the end of third grade. To this end, she presents a report on her findings to the board regarding the execution of the action steps as evidence to support her goal completion in the final evaluation.

When the final board document is prepared summarizing her performance for the academic year, the board mentions math as being a key priority for the upcoming year to match the work and efforts being undertaken to support reading. However, by the time the superintendent receives her final evaluation, the budget has been developed, staffing levels decided, and there is little wiggle room to begin to address this new priority. Having a midyear conference where math could have been identified as a priority area earlier in the budget development process would have been more appropriate and fair to supporting success momentum in the upcoming school year.

There is power in conversation and relationship in truth. Midyear discussions promote assurances that both sides of the appraisal equation have a balanced opportunity to be informed and engage in meaningful exchanges well before the year is complete.

Final evaluations are also a longitudinal piece of institutional memory. The formats that range from checklists, rubrics with accompanying rating scales, and summative narratives are all examples of how the superintendent of schools performance is documented. How the production of the final evaluation is managed—and perhaps equally important, the sentiments about the process by both the board and the superintendent—emerge as major contributors to the sense of efficacy regarding the completion of this work.

The conversations between a board and superintendent are central to the sense of the process.

- Is the document shared ahead of conversation about its contents?
- Is the document read by the superintendent with board members watching their initial reactions in the room?
- Does the superintendent get to have a conversation with the whole board about the evaluation or only board leadership?
- If the conversation is only with the board leadership, how is the superintendent's reaction to the document shared with the rest of the board?
- What if the superintendent disagrees with the evaluation in whole or part; how does the navigation of this subtext unfold?
- Is the evaluation rating(s) subject to public disclosure?

Maintaining mutual trust and respect is perpetually at stake throughout these scenarios. Each of these situations potentially may play a leading role in institutional memory. The professional dialogue born from this process are indelible moments in the board–superintendent relationship. How information is derived and delivered by the board to the superintendent speaks volumes about the nature of the relationship, as is the power that communication has in creating impressions that outlast an evaluation cycle and feed the process in the years ahead.

Chapter Three

Communication, Communication, Communication

Mind the Gap

As is the case in any good working relationship, the quality and frequency of communication between the superintendent and board members is critical to the maintenance of shared understandings regarding the evaluation process. Communication is happening all the time. Whether direct or more passive, information is being transferred between the board and the superintendent on multiple fronts.

A listing of the methods of communication a superintendent may be evaluated against is as follows: *tweets, email, weekly updates, board agendas, back-up materials to board agendas, attendance or nonattendance at particular events, phone calls, face-to-face interactions, board presentations, newsletters, articles, correspondence to families and the community, press releases, public presentations; and reports from others to the board about the superintendent's behaviors, moods, or reactions on a given topic.* Each of these mediums can be disrupted by unsubstantiated inferences or misguided criticism.

Effective communication is a key element in the evaluation of the superintendent. "Keeping the board well informed will not only make the board more effective but will also develop board confidence in the superintendent" (Dykes 1965, p. 132). Therefore, the collaborative development and equivalent understanding of the norms and expected protocols for communication play a premier role in the ultimate success of the superintendent.

Envision the following scenario: *A young person in a high school finds himself in a very difficult situation. Things at home are not going so well, he was recently dumped by his girlfriend, and he is generally finding life at school to be unfair. He is upset and easily triggered by comments from staff trying to help him make good choices about going to class on time, and submitting his work. One interaction between a teacher and the student prompts the student to leave class and walk to the principal's office to voice his displeasure about this teacher.*

Upon meeting with the principal and forcefully sharing how upset he is, he mentions committing harm to himself and reveals to the principal that he is depressed. The principal calls the school counselor who evaluates the student and the student continues to fall into a more depressed state. The counselor advises that the student should be evaluated at a hospital that is better able to handle this level of concern.

After attempts to contact the parent fail, an ambulance is called for transport. Dispatch sends two police officers to evaluate the student and the police walk through the building to visit with the student in the counselor's office. As soon as the police arrive on campus, students start asking to go to the bathroom so they can see what is going on, texting each other about what they think is happening, and generally speculating about what having police on campus could mean. The student ultimately comes out of the office and quietly leaves with the police to receive an evaluation at a local hospital.

In this instance, the superintendent has to balance the privacy rights of the student experiencing depression with the fact that students will go home and talk about the police being on campus that day. This occasional building-level episode involving one student can easily be magnified by rumors and innuendo. In the moments following this event, the superintendent must decide how to communicate the situation to the board to ensure they have the facts about what occurred and to thwart any surprises that may leave them unable to say what every superintendent needs the board to truthfully convey a message such as the following: "The superintendent has alerted the board regarding this event. As he/she is the spokesperson for the district, a message will be disseminated from the superintendent's office to the community regarding what occurred in our district today."

The level of communication between the board and the superintendent should be predetermined rather than circumstantial. In other words, there should be agreed upon communication protocols about how and when the superintendent informs the full board regarding an event versus when it is acceptable to solely alert the board president for the purpose of building general situational awareness. There should also be agreement about how regular communication from the board to the superintendent will be facilitated. Many districts use the board president as a conduit for the mutual provision of detailed reporting between and among the superintendent and the full board governance team.

The establishment of norms, expectations, and shared understandings relative to communication must be cooperatively examined by the board and superintendent. Without common presumptions regarding the conveyance of information during regular business operations, and more importantly when matters reach a crisis level, a superintendent may find their communication efforts rated ineffective or poor.

This situation supports the finding of Castallo, Greco, and McGowan (1992, p. 32), who argue that "the working relationship among board members and the superintendent is healthier when both parties discuss and resolve misunderstandings and disagreements." Further, it is healthier when the expectations around communication are developed and known by all parties.

The grass is always greener where it is cared for and watered. Nurturing the investment in the norms that drive agreed upon communication protocols takes time and is developed as the rhythm and relationship between the superintendent and the board of education evolves. Shannon (1989, p. 26) states, "open, two-way communication is vital in avoiding conflict. Whether it is perceived as a formal system or not, every superintendent has some kind of system for communicating with the school board." The challenge then for board trustees and the superintendent is determining whether the systems focused on the exchange of information adequately meet the needs of the board of education and whether that system can endure the evaluation process.

Linking policy to the systems that govern agreed upon communication norms is a reinforcing cycle that can be sustained beyond institutional memory. For example, most local board policy has a section dedicated to the steps associated with onboarding trustees. A review of the communication protocols that have been codeveloped by the board and the superintendent can be included as one of the documents that are incorporated into the onboarding process. Policy statements such as "in the case of emergency situations, the Superintendent's initial contact will be with the board president and action will be taken regarding immediate communication with the rest of the board" or "we agree to avoid words and actions that create a negative impression on an individual, the board, or the district. While we encourage debate and differing points of view, we will do it with care and respect to avoid an escalation of negative impression or incidents" help to frame the relational expectations regarding communication and construct a framework for district governance behaviors (Evelyn 2012, pp. 1–2). Installing communication protocols as part of the mandated steps that are associated with board member orientation is another way to ensure that the nature of interfacing between the board and the superintendent has a documented standard of practice.

Creating multiple opportunities for dialogue is a sure way to continually unite the board and the superintendent regarding communication expectations and reduce the time lapse that can negatively fuel comments that detract from focusing on shared goals. This can be done during goal setting, the midyear conference, or more informal interactions over the course of a school year.

Katz (1993, p. 23) states it well when he held that "friction reduction or elimination may help boards and superintendents focus on issues and problems, rather than on what each sees as the offending behavior of the other, thus freeing them to do the creative and necessary work that they can only accomplish together."

The literature regarding board–superintendent communications is replete with important understandings that augment the relationship (Luehe 1989; Schmitz and Fitch 2001; Thomas 1975; Pitner and Ogawa 1981); however, perhaps the two most critical understandings in communication between board members and superintendents involve avoiding surprises and not leaving any board member feeling bereft in the sharing of information. Human nature may dictate that some board members just "click" better with the superintendent.

Nonetheless, the superintendent must be careful not to fall into the trap of providing uneven amounts of information to individual board members as a result of easier relationships with some governance team members over others. This blunder is a sure way of dividing the board and breaching the trusting relationships that the superintendent should be working to perpetually reinforce.

The ease of communication that comes from feeling a sense of shared purpose or kinship with a particular board member tempts a courtship of reliance on this individual. This may include using this trustee as a sounding board on topics, a heightened comfort level in responding to their questions outside of board meetings, even the development of a more platonic relationship that comes with getting to know their family dynamics. The nuance in this case is the potential blind spot that the superintendent can develop regarding how the variance in this interpersonal relationship may impact other board members.

Even when interactions are innocuous like when the superintendent and an individual board member inadvertently run into one another at a district sporting event, the potential for pitfalls is present. In such occurrences, the superintendent may naturally circle over to say "hello" and the two may end up having a conversation about something as harmless as parking lot issues. When that board member later relays a summary of the conversation with other trustees, they may feel excluded and think that "secret" talks between the superintendent and the initial board member are regularly occurring.

Over time, the inflated perceptions of these happenstance meetings can promote negative feelings among other members of the board. Even though the superintendent may not be aware that these misconceptions exist, the evaluation will reflect comments around a need for increased transparency, communicating with all board members, and perhaps even a low rating regarding communication skills.

Fulbright and Goodman (1999, p. 7) find that a way to mitigate some of these issues is "if one board member asks a question, send the answer to everyone on the board. This keeps everyone on the same page, and ensures you don't appear to be showing favoritism." Of course, a simple strategy that may be employed if one does not want to reference a particular board member might be to write the whole board stating that "a board inquiry was made about . . ." and then state the question and the answer.

The strategy outlined above ensures that the full board is aware of questions being raised by other trustees and allows individual members to be shielded from reactions to their query. Ultimately, as McCurdy and Hymes (1992, p. 32) find, "a breakdown in communication can occur if one member receives information from the superintendent that others do not get, and if it isn't addressed by the superintendent and board, it can be the germ of a problem." In short, perceptions of favoritism or uneven communication are fraught with challenges for a superintendent and awareness of this dynamic helps in their active exchange of information with the board of education.

When communicating with the board, it is also important to recognize that you are often teaching your "audience" as well as providing information. Acronyms, "edu-speak," and reference points, while making sense to the district leader, may only confuse board members relative to a given topic. As

Davidson (1970, p. 31) notes in his advice to superintendents regarding board communications, "refrain from using educational 'jargon.' Pedagogical statements should be reserved for other parts of your professional practice. Your regular communication with trustees is not the time to impress the Board with your educational vocabulary."

Sending out a communique that reads "Due to an uptick in the number of FRPL (free- and reduced-price lunch) and ELL (English-language learner) students at Dunleavy Elementary, the principal will be looking at ELA (English language arts) and math achievement data to better inform the walk-throughs that take place as a result of our APPR (Annual Professional Performance Review) process" invites questions and perhaps confusion by not being straightforward and clear in what is being proposed.

While a statement like this may be easily interpretable to a superintendent, it may require further clarification for the board. It is incumbent upon the superintendent to ensure that the language utilized when working with the board is clear, concise, and accessible. As Fulbright and Goodman (1999, p. 8) posit, "surprises are good for birthdays, but not for board–superintendent relationships."

Freuend (1988, p. 39) writes, "no one likes to be surprised on the job; superintendents should be aware of the issues and decisions that might stir up controversy, so they can alert the board president and then the entire board." And, Blumberg (1985, p. 44) finds that it is indeed the superintendent's job to avoid surprises stating, "the superintendent must make sure your board is fully informed about matters. He can't predict everything that will happen of course, but he needs to convey the sense that he's on top of things." Avoiding surprises with the board, to the extent possible, is a necessary component of being an effective communicator as a school superintendent. A superintendent's ability to predict when management issues need to be communicated to the board improve with his or her general experience in this leadership role and familiarity with a particular community.

There are many scenarios that illustrate opportunities for unexpected information to come to light. This often occurs when there is a lack of agreed upon communication protocols that have been codeveloped by affected stakeholders. This can also happen when the leader is not asking the right questions or when principals and district support staff fail to share information with the superintendent in a timely manner.

Nothing should happen at a transactional level during a board meeting that causes a surprise. The substantive resources provided before the meeting, agenda-setting process, and weekly communication should cover the host of topics scheduled to be discussed. However, even ensuring hearty preparation is not foolproof and sometimes what seems to be a simple question at the board table can derail an entire narrative. This is why it remains critical to have as many questions submitted in advance of the meeting as possible.

The timing of shared information with the board of education is essential. Of equal importance is maintaining a balance between enabling the board to understand what supports are needed to attain district goals and ensuring that the administration has enough time to develop a comprehensive roadmap to achieve these gains. The failure to adequately manage this divide can have unintended consequences. Imagine the following scenario:

A school has been identified as being in need of improvement. The school has been working diligently to examine areas where they could improve, collect data that supports why they are struggling, and identify action steps that could be undertaken by administration to bring the school to a higher academic standing.

The building principal is asked to give a presentation to the board about the identification of the problem, steps that are underway to interpret underlying causes, and the contemplation of preliminary action items to improve the situation. The superintendent tells the principal not to commit to any ideas in his presentation as the situation is in the nascent stages of being analyzed. The superintendent sends the board the academic data, the report of findings, and general information about next steps in preparation for the presentation by the principal.

The principal presents at the board meeting and upon conclusion the board president asks the principal, "Do you have everything you need to solve the problem? Tell us what you need." Knowing the superintendent's directive to be noncommittal, the principal does not answer the question. Instead the principal says the school does not have any definitive plans yet, and that he will have to get back to the board on that question. The tenor of the meeting immediately shifts and the confidence in the principal and superintendent's ability to lead the staff through the necessary improvement efforts is called into question and subjected to increased scrutiny.

Surprises have consequences. They foster misunderstandings, erode trust, and over the longer term lead to broken relationships between the board and superintendent. In the same ways the superintendent should follow communication protocols that avoid board members feeling ill prepared, alternately, a board should be equally committed to a high level of predictability regarding how board meetings will unfold.

Effective communication protocols and engagement in regular communication activities help diminish the announcement of unforeseen revelations during the actual board meeting. Assuredly, some reporting will appear in the performance narrative regarding communication and will have an impact on how the superintendent is viewed as a leader. To some board members, a lack of having the necessary information may demonstrate the superintendent's mishandling of a situation. Furthermore, the board may present a need to make extended inquiries about the superintendent's work products in an effort to get the information they need to make informed decisions.

Davidson (1970) offers advice as to how to handle situations described in the scenario above:

> If an unsatisfactory situation could have been prevented by better planning on the part of the superintendent or his team, the superintendent should benefit from this in planning future meetings. If no amount of preparation could have avoided the situation, the superintendent would do well to forget it and move on to other things. (Davidson 1970, p. 118)

Beyond building an operational framework with the board, perhaps the most vital way of communicating to the governance team and school community is physical presence. The superintendent's visibility at school, district, and community events speaks volumes to a multitude of stakeholders. The attendance of the district leader at these events demonstrates what they value and specific interests that were prioritized from a scheduling perspective. When a superintendent is present, the community interprets that commitment of time as a sign that the occasion and its participants are important. After all, many stakeholders portend to "know how busy" the life of a superintendent truly is.

The foundation of judgments by board members also becomes apparent in the absence of the superintendent at community affairs. Throughout the year, superintendents' choices regarding the acceptance and declination of invitations are all fundamental communications about what is relevant to the office of the superintendent.

As often as possible, the superintendent should share their attendance at district-related functions with the board. This can avoid divergent thinking about the superintendent's level of visibility and demystify the genesis of how the superintendent is making decisions about the dedication of time to this effort. One cannot possibly attend all relevant occasions. However, regular communication and recording attendance at district and community events can be used as a tool to inform the board about visibility during the evaluation process. In this way, misperceptions relative to how the superintendent is spending his or her time are diffused throughout the year.

"Working with their superintendents, boards should deliberately plan for receiving information. The plan should consider the kinds of information, the level of detail, and its conveyance. This is complex but important; it is often ignored" (Smoley 1999, p. 96). The development of systems that support an ideal maintenance of mutually beneficial knowledge between the board and the superintendent cannot be understated.

For example, data overload could just as easily be viewed as ineffective communication as well as what a board might think is a vacuum of information. Taking into account that board members have to find time to fit board service into their everyday lives, providing a tome of reading for them to regularly complete is not likely to yield a high proficiency rating in an evaluation. Further, providing reading on topics that are disjointed or not obviously connected to strategic goals often leads to confusion and a sense of disorganization regarding the direction of the district.

Finding the balance regarding the interchange of professional knowledge, particular facts, and recommendations requires a concentrated effort. Nonetheless, this evenhanded approach to conveying information anchors the construction of viable evidence for both the nature and purpose of communication in the superintendent's evaluation.

"Some superintendents destroy goodwill by assuming an attitude of superiority and by insisting on the right to decide all educational policies" (Bagin, Gallagher, and Moore 2008, p. 92). Overall, this can lead to negative feelings about the superintendent in general. In this case, the nature of the communication becomes the focus of the appraisal conversation rather than the execution of specific improvements positively impacting student outcomes.

The establishment of norms or communication protocols will promote intentionality regarding the exchange of knowledge between the board and superintendent. This will support a culture that values equitable levels of dialogue with all board members. It can also shape a broader frame including the concepts of visibility, professional expertise, and mutually beneficial information. This is a crucial step in advancing more global reflections regarding how these elements converge under the evaluatory heading of "communication."

Konnert and Augenstein (1990, p. 156) find that an effective superintendent "must know what is to be communicated, with whom to communicate, and how to communicate. The superintendent's image is often judged on the basis and of the type and quality of his/her communication." Thus, the onerous for a successful communication strategy falls to the superintendent to not only deploy, but also adapt as the situation and needs of the board change.

As Dykes (1965, p. 133) puts it, "the informational program should be designed to make the board members the best informed people in the community on all educational matters. Every means at the superintendent's disposal should be used in achieving that goal."

A standard means of communication that brings value to the board–superintendent relationship is found in the weekly update. A weekly update is a helpful way to document the occurrences of the district, to provide board members with information on topics that may be forthcoming in board agendas, and to summarize meetings and activities that have or will take place in the close future.

A weekly update also creates a log over the span of a school year that a superintendent can reference as midyear or final evaluations draw near. Such existing narratives could help defuse comments from board members such as "I was never told about this" and "I don't recall you ever mentioning . . . ."

This documentation also serves as a stopgap thwarting claims like these from dominating conversation during the evaluation process. Furthermore, the weekly update provides an official record that board members can indirectly utilize when they encounter public inquiry about the district and superintendent. Moreover, dovetailing the weekly update with board agendas allows the outline of these public meetings to serve as checkpoints when the board reviews the pursuant work of the superintendent within a given school year. An example of how this would work is when the superintendent writes the following in a weekly update to the board:

At the next board meeting, I will present a proposed budget development calendar. This calendar outlines the work that our administrative team will undertake over the coming months regarding literacy, technology-based initiatives, facilities upgrades, and student safety. At each of the board meetings delineated in the calendar, a presentation will be given to help provide insight with respect to the funding requests. The request for these financial resources will be accompanied by adequate data that demonstrate the need for the program or proposed reduction. If you have any further topics you wish to have explored in this year's budget cycle, we can discuss them at the board table prior to adopting the budget calendar.

As each topic is discussed over the ensuing board meetings, the superintendent ensures that the agenda reflects the scheduled topics and the board is provided with the requisite data to make an informed decision. In fact, it is the commitment to this purposeful alignment that makes the piggybacking of information between weekly updates and board meetings incredibly powerful. It scaffolds the work over an entire school year and serves as a source of data that should inform the final evaluation product.

Another way to ensure official recordkeeping of shared information is to carefully review and read board minutes. Although this work is typically completed by the board or district clerk, sometimes the board meeting minutes inaccurately reflect a particular sentiment or demonstrate a need for clarification. The superintendent may not need to include this in his or her regular practice, however, this review will become particularly essential on occasions when meetings become overly contentious or there are an unusually high number of questions raised about new initiatives within the district. Reading these minutes and understanding how they portray a discussion also provide the superintendent with information points to build upon over successive meetings should the need arise.

There was a Massachusetts politician named Martin Lomasney, who was a political boss at the turn of the last century. Among many things, Lomasney is famous for the quote "Never write if you can speak; never speak if you can nod; never nod if you can wink." While the vitreous nature of this sentiment is questionable, there is something practicable in this statement for superintendents.

Committing particular details such as budgetary figures and statistical data to writing has a very permanent attribute. Freedom of information laws allow members of the public to request the review of correspondence and relative documents. Therefore, written documentation should be thoughtful and measured in both tone and word choices. Remember, the superintendent is not writing to their peers or friends in official updates, and board meeting agendas are a reflection of the service of a municipal corporation.

When speaking, superintendents must also consider their audience and the idea that their words are going to be retold. Like the old game of telephone, the story of how information was delivered will become grander and distorted the more people retell it. A nod is an affirmation technique that may indicate agreement to some folks and a disposition of thoughtful listening

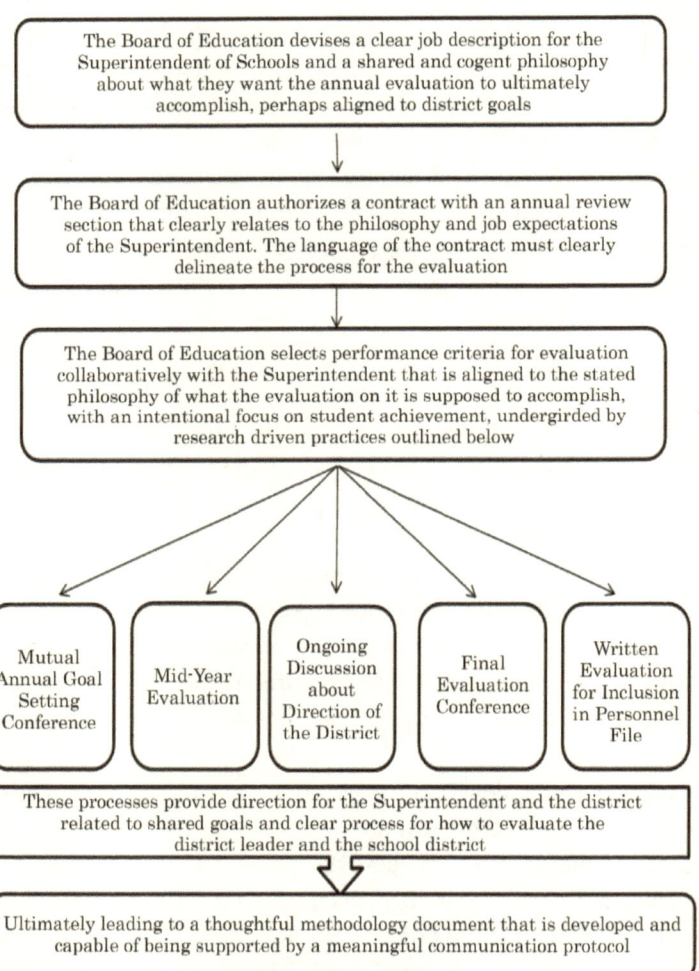

Figure 3.1. Suggested methodology for evaluating the school superintendent.

and acknowledgment to others. Superintendents should be cognizant of their body language when addressing and attending to the public as these nonlinguistic signals could be wrongly interpreted by board members and other constituents.

In our time as district leaders, we have often heard experienced superintendents quip that "paranoia is a skill set." When the superintendent is in the room, it is not uncommon that he or she is center stage or the main attraction. This increased magnetism exponentially promotes the allure of being mundanely judged on attributes that may not be closely linked with effective district leadership. The personal appearance of the superintendent from grooming standards to fashion choices, even the type of car they drive, can become powerful signals that transmit a perceived level of professionalism and value system(s).

It is perilous for a district leader to be unaware of these factors and how such workaday aspects may come to inform an evaluation of their leadership style by the board of education. Indeed Powers (2017) finds that health and vitality, appearance, enthusiasm, speech and voice, communication style, personal qualities, and self-reflection all are attributes that boards have been known to evaluate a district leader upon.

As illustrated in figure 3.1 (on the previous page), the superintendent and board must devise a meaningful evaluation process that is supported by shared expectations regarding the multifaceted dimensions of "communication." Effective communication should ultimately be understood by a board and superintendent as paramount to any relational and evaluative understanding. Without crystalized communication expectations, the construction of an evaluation process lacks a secure foundation and is predictably unreliable.

Chapter Four

"Standard" of Leading

Standards serve as a benchmark for examining professional practice against a normed set of expectations. For superintendents, these standards are the foundational elements of leadership and viewed as quality indicators for the skills and values that should be exhibited by the chief executive officer of school districts.

These standards of practice have sometimes been neatly pared down into demonstrable categories of performance and presented as rubric-based tools purposed for the evaluation of the school superintendent. As is the case with most categorically driven rubrics, performance ratings are usually delineated along a continuum of measures that have equivalent ranges from ineffective to highly effective.

Practicing superintendents are faced with a gamut of conditional situations that cannot easily be measured by mutually exclusive categories and corresponding rating criteria. Furthermore and quite naturally, board awareness of standards for professional practice of school superintendents is often overshadowed by local issues and workaday concerns.

In a limited study of standards and board-driven superintendent search criteria, Ramirez and Guzman (2003, p. 34) find that "school board members valued those standards that emphasized transactional leadership skills to a much greater extent than the standards that focused on transformational leadership qualities." It is important to think about how this dynamic is playing out during the current era of governmental reforms. Public school leaders are required to act as revolutionaries prepared to regularly steer the entire organizational ship in wholly new directions on a regular basis.

Transactional leadership is marked by a relational give and take that maintains conditions of rewards and consequences. For example, those individuals credited with the progression of organizational goals are usually awarded with contract renewal or an increase in their overall compensation. To the contrary, transformational leadership is defined by actions that are rooted in a passionate desire to affect systemic change that in most cases promotes equitable opportunities that build both student and educator capacities to learn.

If the organization of superintendents' performance rubrics are centered around those leadership traits that are not well correlated with leading change, what inclinations will boards adopt when faced with evaluating the more navigational or transformative leadership style versus district management that maintains the status quo? In other words, are rubrics utilized in the evaluation of the superintendent actually building the capacity of the board to engage in a comprehensive evaluation process of the demands placed on modern day superintendents? Simply put, this cannot be true of superintendents' evaluation rubrics that are implicitly biased by their construction to measure the more static conventions of management styles.

The complex duty of adequately preparing globally competent students for the academic, technological, and social–emotional challenges ahead of them requires dynamic leadership to distinguish success markers aligned with these competencies. This is the central work of today's superintendents who must actively inspire all who are working within public school districts to create learning environments that are responsive to the demands of the global citizenry.

Currently, evaluation tools utilized to assess superintendents' performance have been created with an eye toward aligning the goals of the board with the work of district leadership. The vitality of these rubric-based tools lies in establishing a tenacious process marked by a strong collaboration between the board and the superintendent. Although the development of these tools has become more evidence-based, boards can still find themselves impaired by having to link analogous language in the rubric to district leaders' decision making and relative actions.

Furthermore, these evaluation tools are static and lack the flexibility to reflect district needs specific to particular regions or contextualized by local issues. Most boards across the country are not trained in the systematic use of rubrics in their board development programs. Instead, these orientations are purposefully customized to help trustees focus on governance issues focused on fiscal responsibility and policy analysis. As a result, board members are perpetually underprepared to evaluate the highest officer in the district through no fault of their own.

The Professional Standards for Educational Leaders outline ten standards that delineate the work expected of district leadership. They include *mission, vision, and core values; ethics and professional norms; equity and cultural responsiveness; curriculum, instruction, and assessment; community of care and support for students; professional capacity for school personnel; professional community for teachers and staff; meaningful engagement of families and community; operations and management; and school improvement* (National Policy Board for Educational Administration 2015).

The American Association of School Administrators outline eight professional standards for school superintendents that include *leadership and district culture; policy and governance; communications and community relations; organizational management; curriculum planning and development; instructional management; human resources management and values; and ethics of leadership* (Hoyle 1993).

While each of these topical headings and their corresponding attributes illustrate the necessary skill sets of school superintendents, a board looking to assess a superintendent's performance against them may not be well served by the sheer number and composition of the rating categories. The underdeveloped capacity of board members to holistically review the superintendent's work products as the sum of its parts is exemplified by the conflict that can surface in rating a superintendent's performance utilizing a standardized evidenced-based rubric.

On a warm June afternoon, immediately following the graduation ceremony, the board president and vice president asked the superintendent if he had a moment to discuss his final evaluation for his first year on the job. The superintendent, coming off the thrill of his first graduation ceremony as the district's leader, obliged as he was confident of the work that he had done since arriving in the district last fall. After all, in just under a year, he had uncovered urgent matters that needed attention and had begun to make real plans for moving the district forward. The board president presented the evaluation to the superintendent in a folder as they all sat in his office.

The superintendent opened the folder and found that he was rated developing in some of the category headings: community relations, district results, and administration. As he scanned through the rubric, his shock at the rat-

ings provided first turned to disappointment, and then a form of quiet resentment.

All the positive energy that came with closing out the year evaporated in that moment. He had just minutes to review the document and process the emotions and the range of questions cascading through his mind. "Do they really think I am developing? Why didn't anyone tell me I wasn't doing enough? How is this possible, I worked so hard this year, and this is what they think of me? This is not indicative of the feedback that I've been getting all year from my parents and members of the community!"

At the very last page of the evaluation, there was a two-sentence paragraph that followed the summary ratings: "We are very pleased with what has been accomplished. We view this as an extremely positive evaluation. You set high goals and have accomplished them. We are proud of the amount of work you have done in the short time that you have been with us."

The post-evaluation conference immediately followed. "Thank you for this evaluation," said the superintendent. "I am however, very confused. I'm unsure how you've rated me developing in these categories. There are just check marks on a rubric and no description as to why people feel this way. Can you give me some feedback?"

The board president responded, "This is our first year using this rubric and we don't really like it. We think it constrains us in our thinking and it makes us try to fit what you do into boxes. You have been with us for just about a year and that is not a lot of time for us to find you proficient or exemplary in all of these categories. We need more time to evaluate your progress on these fronts. But, this is the rubric and standards we agreed to use this year. This is why we included the sentence about how we think this is a good evaluation."

More confused than ever, the superintendent finished the conference and went home wondering what had just happened and concerned that normative standards in the absence of consideration of local needs and issues had just caused the board to literally "box him in" the developing category.

Hoy and Miskel (2008) argue that rubric-based evaluation models are constrained by the given evaluation criteria, the opportunities to demonstrate expectations dictated by the language of the evaluatory tool, and ultimately, the capacity of the school district to achieve the desired outcome in regard to its organization. The level of staffing, locational distance between school facilities, and management models are all factors that directly influence the success momentum of the board's organizational goals.

Ultimately, the superintendent must facilitate the development of a unified vision that can be translated into thoughtful policies and relative educational practice. This is the necessary precursor to action-oriented steps that enable school boards to operate with high degrees of efficacy.

"Effective school boards commit to a vision of high expectations for student achievement and quality instruction and define clear goals toward that vision" (Dervarics and O'Brien 2011, para. 15). Additionally, these footholds assure that the role of the superintendent appropriately supports and guides the service of the board in ways that bolster their sense of feeling valued and respected as partners in the achievement of board and district goals.

At the intersection of standards and practices is a dialogue about how the role of these calibrated objective measures guides the superintendent's professional behavior, and how the district's premiere instructional leader symbolizes these quality indicators in their direction of the district and partnership with the board of education. During the development of board goals, a review of professional standards may not routinely be included in the discussion. This passive omission can limit the aspirations of superintendent leadership to completing local benchmarks rather than meeting broader standards demonstrating efficacy of leadership.

Moreover, competing interests and the circumstantially opaque meaning of standards thwart the ability of district leaders to hit their mark: "If a target is not reachable, it ceases to be a guide. If the measures to be developed lead to less ambitious definitions of the indicators than the current wording connotes, then the standards being proposed should be thought of as a draft. If not all must be attained, which ones are unnecessary?" (Hawley 1994, para. 6).

Thus, boards are charged with interpreting professional standards of practice for the superintendent, setting their local goals and priorities, and somehow navigating this terrain amid a threshold of other dictates and community interests. The normative expectations of a community to see results-driven performance by district leadership can be found somewhere in between promulgated leadership standards and reality. Additionally, the need for superintendents to justify the identification of budgetary priorities also impacts the broader design of the process that school boards utilize in the evaluation of the district leader.

School boards must be mindful of becoming over reliant on standardized rubric-based evaluation tools when planning for annual performance expectations of the superintendent. While professional standards should certainly share a distinct place in the board's development of goals associated with quality indicators of district leadership, concerted attention must also be directed toward the quality of the superintendent's statement of annual professional goals. It is this document that weaves the strategic alignment of the board and superintendent's targeted outcomes throughout the organization to support a district's continuous improvement efforts.

In the board's review of the superintendent's goals, the partnership must work to mutually identify how the goals will be prioritized, agree upon timelines for progress updates, and define completion rates to ensure a shared regard for sequencing the most urgent concerns. When undertaken as a collaborative process, creating these goals will enable authentic conversations to occur and allow for the identification of key district initiatives to unfurl from all parties on the superintendent–board governance team.

What follows is a sample set of professional goals that were devised to include five categories: student achievement, organizational capacity, budget development, communication and community engagement, and facilities that are authentic to a superintendent's annualized performance expectations.

Professional Goals

- For Superintendent for the XX School Year
- District Mission Statement: District XX will expect and enable our students to . . .
- Vision Statement: All of the children in District XX will learn at the highest levels.

Target Area: Student Achievement

Goal: Provide leadership for implementing high quality curriculum and instruction to promote improved student success.

Means

1. Collaborate with board trustees, administration, and staff to review systems of operations district wide

2. Collaborate with executive- and building-level administration to develop district- and building-level plans in response to new school safety plan guidelines
3. Collaborate with executive- and building-level administration to develop consistent, district-wide Curriculum, Instruction, Assessment (CIA) Plan
4. Develop and implement project management charters to execute a plan that aligns existing K–12 curriculum with the state learning standards including social studies and science
5. Modify common assessment matrix for K–12 to develop an assessment model inclusive of new K–6 curriculum-based assessments for math and English language arts (ELA)
6. Evaluate the use of data to modify and improve curriculum and instructional practices and collaboratively implement recommended shifts
7. Evaluate the implementation of response to intervention (RtI) processes and collaboratively implement recommended shifts
8. Enlist technical assistance from XX professional organization to evaluate targeted instructional delivery models (i.e., special services, reading, and math) and collaboratively implement recommended shifts
9. Establish district curriculum committee to assist in the evaluation of our core programs' ability to meet the needs of all learners and educators
10. Facilitate the continuation of a strategic planning process that identifies long range goals for "teaching and learning" along with impact on facilities with the board and members of the larger school community
11. Review/develop policy that supports increased rigor and relationship building with students and families (e.g., homework, extra help, co-curricular opportunities)
12. Review use of current digitized resources that support tier 1 reading and math instruction

Deliverables

1. Balanced assessment matrix for ELA and math K–6
2. District-wide agreement among educators for common instructional components of a K–6 balanced literacy program

3. Comprehensive plan to improve primary math and ELA curriculum and instruction in the district (e.g., standards-based curriculum, professional development plan, bank of resources, instructional issues)
4. All K–12 teachers will use results of common assessments as discussion points during grade level and common planning time to guide necessary modifications to curricular and instructional practices
5. All administrators will have completed required observations providing valuable feedback by the end of the XX school year
6. District- and building-level improvement plans that forge positive shifts in student achievement data
7. Curriculum and instructional gaps that are not meeting rigor and relevance associated with the CIA Plan will be identified and related opportunities for job embedded professional development will be recommended
8. Identification of resources and provision of rationale for addition of human capital to provide oversight for informational and instructional technology, data management and reporting, business and operations, and human resources

Strategic Outcomes

1. Improvement in reading/ELA performance for all District XX students by three to five percentage points, including underperforming groups by XX month/year
2. Increase in teacher engagement in targeted professional development; specifically, twenty teachers will participate in leadership and innovation zones by the end of the XX school year
3. Goals for high-achieving students will be identified after conducting analysis of trend data by XX month/year
4. Presentation of rationale and job description for recommended increases in human capital by XX month/year.

Target Area: Organizational Capacity

Goal: Provide leadership to increase the percentage of students reading proficiently, effectively reducing segregated special service delivery models, and promoting more inclusive learning environments district-wide.

Means

1. Enlist technical assistance from professional organization XX, auditing instructional delivery models
2. Collaboratively review data collected and recommendations from professional technical support XX
3. Develop shared definition and understanding of inclusion by District XX educators
4. Align resources with accountability targets
5. Develop and implement schedules that support more inclusive practices
6. Identify professional development needs of District XX educators relative to co-teaching, differentiated instruction, new program initiatives, use of instructional technology, and other curricular areas

Deliverables

1. Develop district plan reflecting more inclusive instructional practices
2. Professional development for District XX Educators to promote shared understanding of Valley Stream's inclusive education model
3. Implement scheduling models that promote inclusive practices
4. Create a Professional Development Plan that supports successful implementation of co-teaching, differentiated instruction, new program initiatives, use of instructional technology, and other curricular areas

Strategic Outcomes

1. Realize a three to five percent reduction in the number of initial referrals to special education by September XX
2. Realize a three to five percent increase in the number of SWD accessing general education curriculum K–6 by September XX
3. Realize a three to five percent reduction in the number of students mandated for tier 2 academic intervention services (AIS) by September XX
4. All students with special services will access programs support beginning the first day of school in the XX school year
5. Implement use of mobile learning devices in third and fourth grades

Target Area: Budget

Goal: Provide leadership to promote equitable and increased access to state-driven and local funding and align resources within current budget to maintain high quality academic and cocurricular programs for all students.

Means

1. Collaborate with the board of education to prioritize effective strategies to access equitable and increased access to state-driven and local funding
2. Collaborate with the board to edify the community regarding the impact of the bond project on budget and school taxes
3. Collaborate with the board of education to develop strategies that promote community engagement and garner support from local officials (e.g., Friday open office hours beginning XX month, town hall meetings, inviting the public to board work sessions)
4. Collaborate with executive and administrative teams to align existing resources with targeted student achievement goals
5. Increase professional expertise related to the development of school budget for superintendent and administrative team(s)

Deliverables

1. Tiered approach to budget projections for XX school year
2. Attendance at the statewide school finance consortium conference
3. Increased engagement and support by broader school community in budget process
4. Develop awareness and support for bond proposal by XX month/year

Strategic Outcomes

1. Development of budget that maintains high quality curricular and cocurricular programs
2. Successful capital project vote XX month/year
3. Successful budget vote XX month/year
4. Budget process that positively engages District XX educators and broader school community
5. Alignment of resources with targeted goals for student success

Target Area: Communication and Community Engagement

Goal: Provide leadership to promote effective communication and community engagement.

Means

1. Communicate shared vision that focuses on continuous improvement
2. Be visible in schools and broader school community
3. Meet with all educators and support staff
4. Meet with representatives of community organizations, particularly those with existing partnerships
5. Meet regularly with district-level PTA group and facilitate book study XXX
6. Create culture that fosters community partnerships, recognition, and participation
7. Develop project management charter for review and restructuring of district website

Deliverables

1. Develop and execute identifiable system for broad recognition of excellence in school community
2. Conduct structured meetings with all members of formal leadership team
3. Conduct structured meetings with leadership from all unions
4. Review and restructuring of district web presence
5. Research and develop proposal for adoption of digitized system of gauging, reviewing, and responding to community concerns, questions, and praise
6. Shared understanding and commitment by ninety percent of District XX educators to a district-wide vision focused on continuous improvement using three critical lenses: development of high quality curriculum, leadership and innovation, and systems thinking

Strategic Outcomes

1. Successful opening day highlighting district vision and targeted plans for continuous improvement
2. Eliminate grievances submitted by all unions

3. Meaningful participation by District XX educators in district-wide committees
4. Increased rate of presentations by students and educators at board and faculty meetings
5. Convene annual board of education ceremonies highlighting excellence throughout school community
6. Implement digitized tool to gauge, review, and respond to community concerns, questions, and praise

Target Area: Facilities

Goal: Provide leadership to ensure successful outcomes to facilities improvement efforts.

Means

1. Successfully market capital improvement work to XX school community
2. Consistently monitor and evaluate capital project work
3. Regular attendance at all meetings related to capital project
4. Regular walkthroughs of accessible areas of construction
5. Regular meetings with construction manager and facilities director
6. Regular meetings with architects, construction manager(s), financial advisors
7. Evaluate/monitor district-wide preventative maintenance plan
8. Evaluate/monitor work order system(s)

Deliverables

1. Successful capital project vote on XX
2. Secure contractual partnership with public relations firm
3. Regular updates from administration, architects, and construction managers at board of education meetings
4. Provision of critical information sharing to board of education in Friday updates

Strategic Outcomes

1. Completed projects in phase I that are on time and within two percent of budgeted projections or under budget

2. Digitized preventative maintenance (PM) plan that operates systemically
3. Work order turnaround time reduced by fifteen percent

> Today's school boards are sensitive to the public's tendency to credit or blame them for school district matters related to curriculum, budget, even the school district's daily operation. Such issues are often misinterpreted by newspapers and misunderstood by the public. And, although boards are aware of the distinctions between their policy-making responsibilities and administrators' responsibilities to implement policy, they still feel the need to reassure their constituencies that they are doing a proper job. How do school boards prove they are accountable? (Edwards 1988, p. 117)

Effective school boards demonstrate their regard for community traditions by representing these norms in discussions about how the district's students should be educated. "Effective school boards have a collaborative relationship with staff and the community and establish a strong communications structure to inform and engage both internal and external stakeholders in setting and achieving district goals" (Dervarics and O'Brien 2011, para. 15).

The school board's devotion to predicating their service upon community-wide principles is foundational to student learning outcomes and provides a schema for the superintendents' understanding of his or her performance expectations. Divergent norms, disparate thinking, and one-offs at the board table consume time, energy, and resources as a superintendent attempts to meet the needs of rogue ideas or factions of board members.

The job of the superintendent is to understand the will of the board as a collective. This is more difficult to know without the board's prior commitment to purposefully defining their underlying beliefs and values as the district's governance team. Further, if the design of the performance expectations are reflective of contemporary concerns rather than meaningful standards, then as Ramirez and Guzman (2003, p. 37) find "it might be natural for a school board to emphasize what they need for the future, what they perceived they lacked in their prior superintendent or what they value as good leadership based on their collective knowledge base."

Patterson (2003) notes that it is the stability of values in an organization that helps it advance over the course of time, and successive superintendents and boards aligned toward common values produce the greatest degree of efficacy in promoting student learning and achievement. School boards generally operate and exist to develop policy. "Effective school boards are accountability driven, spending less time on operational issues and more time focused on policies to improve student achievement" (Dervarics and O'Brien 2011, para. 15).

Well-crafted policy, along with a shared understanding of the organization's values, contributes much to the success of any public school district. As many observers have noted there is in education a natural tension between policy and practice. . . . Hence policy can serve as a helpful goad and stimulus to practice-pressure, [which] as we have seen, is crucial to innovation" (Evans 1996, p. 295). Hence, a board's work is optimal when it has a foundation of collective values and those principles inculcate themselves into the organizational policies that advance the work of the district.

Rudolph (Rudy) Crew, former chancellor of New York City Public Schools, in his work *Only Connect* (2007), states that for a school board to be effective it must be unified, able to problem solve, be focused, have the ability to engage the community to support the work of the district, and have a "dogged persistence, unfailing devotion to outcomes, a clarity of purpose, and respect for expertise" (Crew 2007, p. 204).

How agenda items are developed, information is shared and openly communicated, and the manner in which the board and superintendent wield their authority all have a veritable impact on the public's perception of the relationship between the superintendent and the school board. These are also critical signs that lead the public's sense about how effective the governance team can be in achieving the goals sustained by the organizational mission. Overall, the sentiments regarding these factors will strongly influence the board's approach to the superintendent's evaluation process.

Houston and Eadie (2002, p. 4) warn against the traditional governance nature of boards to be "passive-reactive" in their operational design. They argue that boards that are operationally designed to behave in this way demonstrate little to no leadership over the organization and as a result, lack the ability to make long-term gains as a board toward advancing the common mission of the district. They contend that it is the superintendent who shares a great responsibility in helping the board increase its facility by designing opportunities to actively leverage board members into the work and successes of the district.

Houston and Eadie (2002) further argue that by highlighting and showcasing the work of the board and its members, superintendents can cultivate greater senses of organizational unity. However others, like Carver (2006) are not as convinced that the role of the chief executive officer (CEO) should be to bring about board cohesion. He argues, "only a deluded board waits for its CEO to make it a good board" (Carver 2006, p. 189). Accordingly, he believes that it is the board itself that is responsible for its own successes as a governing body.

The disharmony described by Houston and Eadie (2002) and Carver (2006) is more pointedly explained as the balance that superintendents work toward to engender goodwill among board members. This egalitarian tightrope can be temperamental as it is distributed across five to nine member boards that are representing as many constituencies throughout the school community.

Nonetheless, this is the pathway to a ubiquitous regard for the superintendent's leadership, and concomitantly what a board must shoulder to unify effective governance operations. This cohesion increases the board's efficacy in governing situations that are hindered by forces attempting to derail the superintendent's ability to meet targeted expectations.

While goals directly support the mission of an organization, it is important to distinguish the essence of goals versus priorities. In theory, goals can be accomplished. Priorities have an immediacy that is based in value judgments supported by goals. The participation of the board in augmenting performance standards should happen during the goal-setting process. This requires a time commitment from board members to understand the needs of the district, concerns of their constituencies, and the ability of the superintendent to communicate and accomplish assigned tasks.

Moving from priorities to goals requires a focused endeavor on the part of school boards. There is a true difference between board goals and priorities. Some may argue that priorities cannot be accomplished but are rather a point of continuous focus, whereas goals are actually capable of being accomplished.

Take, for example, the notion of achieving equity as it relates to student participation rates in instrumental music. Philosophically, equity could be deemed a priority by the board of education; however, the equity goal must have practical applications such as ensuring that all students who wish to play a musical instrument have access to the program regardless of their family's ability to pay for a rental instrument or the district's provision of transportation to low income families for high-level music-related events. The power dynamic regarding the give and take between the board and the superintendent is also a significant variable in final goal setting for the district.

As Mountford (2004, p. 737) notes, "it is important for board members and superintendents to be given opportunities during board development sessions, and within educational leadership preparation programs, safe forums to carefully examine, in an honest and self-reflective manner, their motivations and conceptions of power." Goal setting; standards; and priority identification by the full board, individual members, and the superintendent carry multiple opportunities for power maneuvers. If the pervasive authority of these dynamics is not openly discussed, these external forces have the potential to simmer until an evaluation of the superintendent causes slow disagreements to boil over.

Designing a collaborative methodology that focuses on goal setting is an inherent step for boards and superintendents to build transparency and trust into the appraisal process.

Late summer and into the fall, the board of education meets for a few hours before each board meeting to outline their goals for the year. At the opening goal-setting meeting, each board member has the floor to share their ideas, performance targets, and concerns about the direction of the district.

Board members listen intently to the issues and use this time to converse with one another about what they are seeing, and their hopes for the district moving forward. Since structured board meetings rarely allow for board members to process what each is thinking about on a personal level, this process also has the potential to help board members understand the perspectives of one another. Using chart paper, all the board members comments are recorded.

At the next meeting, the comments are distilled through discussion into subject headings (priorities) such as safety, academics, facilities, social/emotional health, and equity. These headings then become departure points for even larger conversations as to how the ideas on the chart paper can be refined into board-supported goals. Not every idea on the chart paper makes it into a goal, and not every comment is capable of being actualized into a goal, in terms of it being a measurable, observable, and achievable task. These conversations sometimes carry over into multiple board meetings as data requests are made and information is refined to inform the goal-setting process.

Once general consensus is reached, the board goals become the framework for the work of the district and the superintendent as he or she devises their annual goals for the year. Each year thereafter, the notes of the previous goal-setting process are reviewed, priorities are evaluated, and either continuing goals or new goals are set and expanded upon. Further, this collaborative process allows for all voices to be heard and contributes to a sense of shared ownership of the goals and stabilizes priorities over time.

The refinement of goals and forward progress also brings elements of change. One of the insights that a standards-based evaluation tool does not always present is the formidable components of leading transformative actions. At its core, change is fraught with the emotion, capacity, and the systemic underpinnings of any organization.

When new ideas, values, and innovative ways of thinking are injected into the status quo, systemic opportunities are born that engender new operational pathways within an organization. Undergirding the change movement, however, are conditions and people that are indeed comforted by doing what has always been done.

Disturbing a static foundation unnerves those best served by the current ways of doing things. In the case of educational organizations, the desires of those wishing to maintain the existing state of affairs must be consistently informed by facts that are vested in data. Moreover, the introduction of diverse perspectives cannot be so disruptive that the value of an idea becomes overridden by those who cannot envision how the change can feed organizational advancement.

Examining the superintendent's goals through the lens of practice-driven standards serves to professionalize the evaluation process and can strengthen the relationship with the board of education. Although the district will have some history relative to past changes, the employment of standards-based criteria for evaluating outcomes can help the board engage in a more forward-thinking approach that is anchored by quality indicators of leadership behavior.

This methodology can also promote a more concerted understanding of the comprehensive plan that must be executed for large-scale change. Using the example of professional goals included in this chapter, visualize a goal being developed under the target area of budget with the identified priority of increasing economic efficiency by closing a school and building an extension on to an existing building.

While on the surface the goal may seem clear, there are a multitude of action steps that must be executed to even begin to think clearly about this work. These should be included in each of the five broad categories listed as follows: student achievement, organizational capacity, budget, communication and community engagement, and facilities. Every aspect of this monumental endeavor can be outlined using this format.

Each of these subcategories must be included in the statement of professional goals to best facilitate the holistic and granular appraisal discussion that will support the superintendent's overall rating for the school closure. There are evaluatory headings within some rubric-based performance tools that include areas such as vision and leadership, communication, and management of resources.

However, without consensus about the identification of priorities and influence of institutional memory, and established communication protocols, the professional standards are devoid of the necessary foundational underpinnings. In this context, the performance appraisal process becomes dominated by rubric-based tools without a professional plan having the potential result of evaluating issues that were not central to the district and superintendent's annual goals.

Not every change is pioneering nor does every change work to best serve an organization. Indeed, not every change foments an energy that transforms an organization for the better. The successful leadership of change is how it comes to be described as transformative. Change that is poorly communicated, disorganized, and lacks fidelity will cause some board members to become dispossessed from the superintendent. Other trustees may begin to question the integrity of leadership and the superintendent's capacity to affect meaningful change. Worse yet, there can be board members that are eager to exploit the missteps of district leadership to achieve alternative goals.

Considering the pace of transformative innovations in contemporary society, honing leadership skills to direct and facilitate this visionary work has become imperative. For school systems that are mired in the traditions of the agrarian cycle, change is constantly at the superintendent's doorstep.

Superintendents that are leading districts in their first year may find themselves submitting bold criticisms to the board about parts of the overall educational programming. Their efforts to put some quick "wins" up on the board and their willingness to take risks that seek to improve their assessment of immediate organizational needs often puts them in a precarious position. This is particularly true when the relational foundation of the evaluation process marked by trust and mutual respect between the board and the superintendent has not been firmly established. As Jentz and Murphy (2005) note,

> Disoriented, but under intense pressure to "do something—and fast," these administrators buy into the conventional view that bold leaders hit the ground running. Feeling whipsawed, yet wanting to please, they reflexively hide their confusion and try to appear decisive by acting quickly. In so doing, they often sour their honeymoon. (Jentz and Murphy 2005, p. 738)

Accordingly, the challenge to move quickly on the part of the board or superintendent to improve learning outcomes for students brings fierce energy that can be difficult to wield. Strong leaders have both the courage and confidence to attend to details related to institutional memory and the goal-setting process, thereby avoiding the potential for the celebration of a "quick win" to be undercut by complaints that reveal themselves as part of the evaluative narrative.

Kotter (1996, p. 165) argues that, "because management deals mostly with the status quo and leadership is primarily associated with change, in the next century, we will have to become much more skilled at creating leaders. Without enough leaders, the vision, communication, and empowerment that are at the heart of transformation will simply not happen well enough or fast enough to satisfy our needs and expectations."

Evans (1996) argues that stakeholders in educational organizations confront a brutal duality when it comes to change; they must either resist the change effort or find ways to acculturate toward it. However, change brings with it conflicting value sets for different individuals and presents many opportunities that require genuine leadership.

Evans (1996, p. 55) further contends that "the beginning task is to make the case for innovation, to emphasize the seriousness of the problem and the rightness of a solution." Challenging the present conditions to the point of action is something that humans are invariably unaccustomed toward doing. Indeed therefore, Evans (1996, p. 125) holds that "reform can only be built on a platform of trust and consensus."

A key element upon which successful management of a change initiative is developed and trust can be built is managing the flow of information.

Bridges (2009, p. 32) contends that change opportunities often encounter turbulence because "managers substitute a fabrication of half-truths and untruths. Not only do these later turn out to be outright lies, but managers often trip themselves up with inconsistencies and new stories to cover the old inconsistencies."

Indeed, the flow of information can make or break a situation. Bridges (2009, p. 32) holds, "for every week of upset that you avoid by hiding the truth, you gain a month of bitterness and mistrust. Besides the grapevine already has the news, so don't imagine that your information is a secret." Once the rumor mill takes over, or if individuals feel shut out of a process, it tends to engender mistrust, abdication from the process, or create hurt feelings. Thus, articulating why a change is occurring brings with it more opportunities for individuals to feel part of the process.

Bridges (2009, p. 16) writes that "people aren't in the market for solutions to problems they don't see, acknowledge, and understand. They might even come up with a better solution than yours, and then you won't have to sell it, it will be theirs."

To build and establish that trust, a leader must also contend with his own set of emotions, as Patterson (2003, p. 106) posits, "it hurts deeply to bring pain into the lives of others as you ask individuals to abandon what they have known and done for so many years." Patterson argues that it is indeed the leader's responsibility to lead through the temporary pain of transitions for the longer-term value that the change initiative will hold for the organization.

Patterson (2003, p. 81) holds that it is undeniably the stability of an organization that school leaders must aspire toward: "All it requires are people in leadership roles who truly care about the long-term vitality of the organization and who demonstrate their caring by implementing policies to secure 'longer-term' leadership."

Thus, building a case for change is not in and of itself alone a sufficient reason for implementing change. The change must be based upon not only trust between an educational leader and his community, but also upon a long-term strategy to ensure that the anguish a community may feel as a result of the change is necessary to bring stability and continuity to the organization in the years ahead. The change must also be predicated upon the organization's culture.

Hoy and Miskel (2008, p. 214) define the organizational culture as the "shared set of orientations that holds a unit together and gives it a distinctive identity. Culture can be examined in terms of shared assumptions, shared beliefs and values, or shared norms." Furthermore, change is not a single variable that can be isolated and contained; it permeates multiple attributes of an organization and either reflects or disrupts the cultural behaviors existent in the school community.

Bolman and Deal (2003, p. 378) argue that "change always creates division and conflict among competing interest groups. Successful change requires an ability to frame issues, build coalitions, and establish arenas in which disagreements can be forged into workable pacts." If a leader does not generate such a framework, or if people cannot understand how a decision was reached, the opportunity exists for unrest to disrupt the change paradigm and for people to feel a sense of removal from the overall change process.

Bolman and Deal (2003, p. 380) further contend that "any significant change in an organization triggers two conflicting responses. The first is to keep things as they were, to replay the past. The second is to ignore the loss and rush busily into the future." When formulating plans to create change, it is essential to let constituencies grieve, to embed mechanisms that promote checkpoints regarding where people are in the process, and to remember that board members and superintendents each need time to recalibrate after letting go and establishing a new normal as a result of the change instigated by goal-setting processes.

America's tidal wave of education reform efforts has led to a culture that naturally promotes goals leading to change during the superintendent's evaluation life cycle. This is apparent in the latest review of ambitious targets set by both boards and superintendents. Aspirational goals set by public school boards project values that in theory work to ensure instructional programs that not only meet but exceed promulgated standards for learning. Many times, these goals are focused on increasing the effectiveness of technology or promoting equitable access to both rigorous academic and extracurricular programming. Developing an understanding for leading change is a necessary component for galvanizing success momentum and empowering public school districts to continue to evolve as learning organizations.

Transformative leaders are often recruited for their penchant and agency for leading change. These experienced CEOs are well acquainted with the fact that a board's familiar decree, "we hired you because you are a change agent," is more than just words. The demands of organizational change may not be fully known to boards, however experienced leaders understand the potentially negative impact of disrupting orthodox structures on the longitudinal service of school superintendents.

"To some degree, the downside of change is inevitable. Whenever human communities are forced to adjust to shifting conditions, pain is ever present" (Kotter 1996, p. 4). Too much change too quickly, whether aligned with board goals or not, places a strain on traditional systems and causes energy to be expended that is not sustainable in the long run.

Additionally, boards can become fatigued in finding problems, tired of hearing bad news, and weary of being shown ways in which its oversight of the district resulted in tremendous problems and poor systemic practices. The advent of unintended consequences can arise from the overstimulation provoked by excessive change processes.

These ramifications manifest in ways that are counterproductive to highly functioning boards and erode the foundation of a trustful relationship between the board and the superintendent. Primary examples of these downward spiraling scenarios are exhibited when the board wants to be informed of everything and becomes skeptical that it is not getting the entire story. Thus, increasing demands for results in shorter time periods and quick finger pointing to examples of when implementation of new ideas do not unfold exactly as planned. These dysfunctional behaviors evince a generalized feeling that ignores measurable accomplishments and overshadow the evaluation process.

Consider the situation described below.

Mrs. Smith is near the end of her third year of her superintendency in a small city school district. This is her tenth year as a superintendent and she was recruited to her current position because of her reputation as a collaborative leader that has a knack for uniting school communities in support of positive changes for students and their families.

It is the beginning of March and the superintendent and board president begin a casual conversation at the end of their regularly scheduled agenda-planning meeting about how pleased they both are regarding the attainment of the shared goals of the board and the superintendent.

During the conversation, the board president asks the superintendent to review the before and after care program that the district has utilized for some time now. When the superintendent asks how long, the president says he is not sure. He tells Mrs. Smith that he has received complaints about this vendor and that other board members also want her to look into these concerns.

The superintendent calls the longest serving board members who have both served for more than two decades to ask about the vendor. They both share that the district has had other extended day providers and that they have been down this road before. Neither of them indicates that changes to the extended day program presented concerns in the past.

The superintendent asks her principals to visit the programs in their respective buildings over the next week and they all provide reports that contain some level of negative information about the existing programs. These concerns include poor feedback about the staff, the quality of homework help, and a lack of security measures to properly identify adults responsible for picking up the children. Two of the most senior principals report that these problems have existed for "some time."

A week later, the superintendent shares what she learned from her principals with the full board in the executive session. The board asks the superintendent for a recommendation and she suggests that they widen their research of the issue before taking any formal action. The board becomes insistent about taking a more immediate action and the superintendent recommends that they send out a request for proposal (RFP) before the renewal of the annual contract with the current vendor.

At the beginning of the third week in March, the superintendent writes a letter to the school community alerting them about the request for proposal process for before and after care programming. The next day is a board meeting and parents begin mobilizing to attend the meeting to voice their displeasure about the decision to promote the opportunity to review other extended day programs. After all, no one asked them about their level of satisfaction with the current provider.

Didn't the district know that they already sent the current provider the down payment for next year? Was the district oblivious to the fact that if they hadn't sent in the money that they might not be guaranteed a slot for their children?

At the board meeting twenty parents show up. They are very vocal about not being involved in the decision-making process about their children's after care provider and demand that the district delay the RFP process. The board president does his best to manage the parents' angst, but the situation worsens as more parents make comments about feeling left out of the process.

The superintendent can see that at the heart of the issue is an emotional and trustful attachment to the current provider. It is also apparent that although she has built a strong support base in her community, she is on shaky ground with the group of parents at the board meeting.

The superintendent is clear about what must happen. She apologizes to the parents in the room and assures them that she and the board would never engage in a process that would breech their trust or confidence in putting the quality of their children's care first. She pledges to write to them before the end of the week once the board and she have a chance to discuss the information they learned from the parents that evening.

The superintendent calls for a closed session at the end of the meeting where she makes the recommendation to rescind the RFP process stating that it was too late in the year to introduce the prospect of this change. In that moment, the newest board member, who has been a resident of the district for twenty years, states that the current provider has been with the district since she became a member of the community. Another board member agrees with this assessment and adds that he cannot remember there ever being another company providing extended day services.

In the end, the board agrees to delay the RFP process until the following year and asks the superintendent to include a formal review of the before and after care program in the development of her formal statement of professional goals for the next school year. In her final evaluation, the superintendent is encouraged to continue to provide her recommendations to the board of education as had been her practice. The board also included that the timing of any recommendation becomes a major factor in the successful implementation of these recommendations.

At first, the superintendent is miffed by what she reads in the evaluation. She tries to unpack exactly what she remembers about how the RFP process unfolded and her annoyance rapidly fades to what she knows too well. Successful leadership must include all the steps that support change initiatives whether they are large or small. And although the urgency of the matter quickly became clear to both her and the board, as the leader she allowed the insistence of the board to dismantle her comprehensive approach to this issue. As a reflective practitioner, she agreed with the board's commentary and assessment regarding the planful schedule of coordinating the RFP process in the future starting with the goal-setting process.

In a healthy working relationship with the board, superintendents should utilize the combination of the goal-setting and evaluation processes to be selective about what needs to be accomplished. The recommendations for future goal-oriented performance often cited in the final evaluation ensure that some of the change initiatives originate from sources outside of the superintendent. This can also help the superintendent sustain the perspective of leadership as a marathon and not a sprint.

Ushering rapid change to a system that is largely static creates the potential to perpetuate initiatives at an unsustainable pace, and leads to having unrealistic expectations about what can occur in a specified time period. Remembering that at times slow is fast, choice is inviting, and data informs decision making allows a free flow of ideas from both the bottom and top of the organizational pyramid.

In summarizing the pitfalls that await leaders during the change process, Patterson (2000) offered the advice below:

> Watch out for rocks in your pocket. If you're doing your job right, eventually you will start accumulating rocks in your pocket from alienating certain groups or individuals because you can't please all of the people all of the time. As you gather the rocks, no single rock may seem at the time particularly heavy ... although I've been known to collect a few boulders right on the spot. Anyway, as you collect the rocks in your pocket, the cumulative weight will start to take you under. (Patterson 2000, p. 32)

Allowing the board or the superintendent to be pulled "under" can be avoided by formalizing a shared process anchored by goal setting. Having goals that are clearly understood by all the parties to the evaluation—which augment normative standards for educational leadership and bring the board and superintendent together around common attributes for district improvement—is a powerful step toward creating an evaluation system that is fair and transparent.

The examination of superintendents' performance through the lens of standards has become particularly fixed in this era of federal statutes that publicly compares student achievement outcomes for schools and districts. Superintendents are constantly evaluated going "all in" on standards-based tools as a methodology for evaluation.

Exclusive utilization of a tool that may be comprehensively examined for the first time in the weeks leading up to a performance review shifts the focus of the evaluation process to documentation and forecloses on rich opportunities for collaboration and discussion. Having these authentic conversations better prepares boards and superintendents to handle the difficult tasks that are part of running a school district.

Envision a process where boards know what they want out of an evaluation process. This would involve jointly selecting the tool and relative evaluation protocols with the superintendent, inviting the superintendent along for the intellectual journey deriving board goals, and the utilization of leadership standards that reflect local concerns and continuous improvement for students' outcomes. Now, leverage this process as a way for districts' CEOs to document their efforts toward meeting the standards and agreed-upon goals that boards can use to provide an overall rating for the superintendents' performance.

While the schema described above would require the alignment of resources, it is time well spent. These fundamental tasks can be accomplished by leveraging language in the superintendent's contract focused on the evaluation process as well as during an initial governance team work session shortly after the superintendent is hired. It is advisable for superintendents that take the helm of districts that experienced a contentious exit of their last district leader, to require this kind of work session in the contractual language. Notwithstanding, good leadership practice suggests that all superintendents that are new to a district consider including verbiage in their contracts that require engagement in shared work sessions that strengthens the evaluation process and provides a communication roadmap. The board and superintendent can use the work products from this critical caucus to navigate goals, identify priorities and relative systemic change, and explore leadership standards as they relate to the evaluatory process of the superintendent.

The goal of successful leadership in the evaluation process is to prevent unspoken concerns from weighing down the cultural shifts that necessarily raise the level of the evaluation to something that is both informative and substantive in its design and feedback. Leadership is about creating the moment. It is about fostering and nurturing the environment that enables effective work to unfold and the future to be created. At the heart of leadership is the capacity to see that the present is only part of the journey and the leader builds the synergy to keep the organization moving toward another part of the story.

Chapter Five

Solstice

The solstice on June 21 represents the annual event of maximum sunlight and conversely, December 21 is the one time a year destined for the least illumination on a day's journey. Solstices mark the beginning of seasons, and like clockwork they are a nonnegotiable predictable occurrence. These fixed hours each year when the sun reaches its highest and lowest points are akin to a good evaluation process.

Calendar markers are a time of celebration and reflection, of setting into motion new plans and activities, and enjoying the bounty of work completion. Without our undivided attention, the solstice always comes as do many other events. There are certainly signs, Seussian interludes like moving-up ceremonies, holiday concerts, and homecomings that balance out the other side of the equation. Nonetheless, the process of the superintendent's evaluation is in constant motion and unavoidable, even when what should be systemic elements may be informal and undocumented.

From the moment the first bus pulls out of the parking lot in September to the days leading up to graduation months later, superintendents are tasked with a broad range of responsibilities. Some of these job-related actions can be categorized as oversight of daily operations, while others require more concerted effort over time to accomplish. Each aspect of this leadership role is characteristically expansive, taking on new dimensions with the review of data-informed expectations each academic year.

From a servant–leader perspective, the work should be rooted in service to a greater good and nested in improving the lives of all children. To move from dutiful tasks that a job represents to something more meaningful requires a vision.

A vision is something that has been internalized, that speaks to aspirational claims, and brings with it energy and a clear sense of why specific decisions must be made. These decisions may end antiquated practices and initiate systemic changes that promote equity and inclusion throughout the district. A vision anchored in shared understandings takes those decisions points and paints them with a more deliberative and purposeful brush. However, generating a vision, cultivating buy-in, and creating actionable plans require getting to both know and understand the culture and climate of the organization.

Novice superintendents know that there are job-related tasks that require daily attention. School administrators have much familiarity with this kind of work. Leadership of the district in its entirety, however, must be more prescriptive to move the organization forward. The development of a quality entry plan that will yield an understanding of the district's current status is an important first step for any superintendent.

A sound entry plan provides an incoming superintendent with several perspectives that can act as snapshots of target areas identified in the professional goals statements: student achievement, organizational capacity, communication and community engagement, budget, and facilities. It should highlight successful aspects of the educational infrastructure and also provide the superintendent with investigatory conversations about what is working well and what is not from a host of varying perspectives.

An entry plan is about data collection. It is an opportunity for the new leader to listen and learn, and perhaps more importantly, reflect about the overall capacity of the organization. The entry plan assesses the needs of the district and provides insights into next steps that could ultimately support a preexisting condition or generate a new vision altogether. The challenge for new district leadership falls in the careful review of the many suggestions for needed improvement, and for the superintendent to treat the entry period as one of genuine learning. During this entry state, it is equally essential that the superintendent guard against making promises and commitments toward effecting general change as they become lasting pledges that the superintendent may have to account for.

The perception that a superintendent needs to establish "quick wins" in order to show that they have the ability to do the job creates an urgency that sometimes thwarts the success momentum that is initiated by building a shared vision. This can happen for a host of reasons notwithstanding, the desire to build some political capital among various constituencies by addressing their concerns, and the eagerness of a new district leader to step out of the shadows of their predecessor.

The degree of efficacy in the execution of an entry plan, in large part, determines the resultant report to the board of education. In fact, the process of this intellectual journey of seeking to learn about district operations circles back to the board well before the superintendent is finished. Preconceived notions about priorities within the district may vary from what the superintendent discovers through the entry process and what the board has been living with over time. How the new district leader marries the concerns in their service to the board and the full school community plays a decisive role in how the board–superintendent relationship evolves in the initial months of a superintendency.

Constructing a shared vision, or at least establishing a mutual regard for the preexisting vision, is difficult work. Board members are sophisticated individuals. They have insights into an organization that a newer leader does not. They also possess a historical perspective that speaks to reasons for how a district operates. At the same time, if board members have not been provided with key information, they may have a distorted sense of operations at the district level and in schools. Further, if their understanding of organizational history is incomplete, the challenge for the new leader is to decide how and when to divulge information that may rattle collective thinking about a given topic.

School superintendents who construct a vision in absentia of their board's input thwart the opportunity to generate this global insight. These new leaders may rightly find themselves mired in questions because of their failure to include communal touch points that a shared vision represents. The process of creating, growing, and supporting a shared vision are key contributors to the annual cycle of superintendent evaluation.

Fostering knowledge about how the district's vision is motivated by a shared purpose sets the district on a distinct course. It demands the development and collection of data to inform the key indicators, collaborative conversations about results-driven goals, and credible opportunities to discover differing perspectives regarding student outcomes.

The pursuit of excellence in any organization requires a sustainable level of discomfort. The development of a formidable vision mandates authentic relationships in which trusting individuals share their hopes and dreams.

Agreed upon understandings between the board and the superintendent about how the vision will be actualized are foundational to this effort.

The leadership of both the board and the superintendent in projecting a unified vision is ultimately manifested in the superintendent's evaluation. If the vision is not jointly held by the board and the superintendent, or if it is developed in isolation, it may be incongruent with the espoused philosophy of the board. In turn, the superintendent's action steps may be viewed as flawed in both their orientation and design. The resultant work product may be deemed superficial and misaligned with the board's expectations. This will result in negatively swaying the evaluation process and painting an awkward picture of the superintendent's efficacy.

After constructing a narrative that is informed by board members and members of the school community, it is essential to gather and collect information from other relative stakeholder groups. This can be achieved by hosting forums, creating surveys, and leveraging social media to ensure access to varying constituencies. Overall, these interactive communication strategies are critical to creating an authentic buy-in. Again, transparency is central to the successful outcomes of this inclusive endeavor.

A preordained vision sans public input will create a limited data collection process that fails to engender goodwill, and perhaps stall the superintendent's ability to address long-term goals of the district. Furthermore, it will be too late to make midcourse corrections once this disconnect becomes evidentiary feedback that drives the evaluation narrative about how the superintendent performed relative to communication and community engagement. A true district vision is derived through an open, collaborative process that is informed by good data and transparent dialogue: a process that keeps the needs of the students at the forefront of all discussions, and at the same times seeks to balance the long-term economic implications of these decisions with priority concerns of the district.

Leadership must energize the conversations that present central information toward achieving the vision. Board members and the superintendent should shoulder this work together to systemically impart and sustain this shared message through potentially difficult reactions of stakeholders. In this way, the superintendent minimizes the political machinations of those who seek to actualize a limited agenda that may not always put children first.

The evaluation of the vision is achieved through the strategic implementation of a continuous improvement plan. Ratings that are derived in conjunction with this plan should be supported by concrete evidence rather than opinion to substantiate the objective nature of the superintendent's evaluation process. When subjective information is included in the evaluation document, it clouds the importance of the district's vision and decreases the power of the evaluation process to generate leadership capacity.

Evidenced-based evaluations are dependent on the ability of the board–superintendent relationship to create a veritable account of the superintendent's annual performance. An indisputable account of leadership activity may also challenge preconceived notions about the district and its condition, and ultimately force a school board to consider its philosophy supporting the superintendent evaluation by revisiting the question: What is the purpose of the superintendent's evaluation process?

School districts are oftentimes organized in ways that represent the values of their individual communities. Programmatic offerings, judgments regarding curricular importance, and possibilities for student engagement in extracurricular activities are evaluated holistically and through the constituent-based lens of board members.

When leaders fail to recognize the disparate views and needs of these individual school communities within broader district plans, they begin to become insulated to both the organization's needs as well as individual or group consensus about their job performance. This lack of objectivity can inadvertently censure authentic listening and often places a leader's credibility in jeopardy. In situations dominated by individuals that are less inclined to challenge those in charge, a leader must have the ability to put their egos aside and genuinely attend to the interpretation of issues that thwart equity, inclusion, and opportunities to grow with the organization in their role as the superintendent of schools.

Beyond simply being aware of the social networks that exist in a school district and how these groups impact opinions about a superintendent's performance, it is imperative that a leader recognize the distinct context of diverse situations. When moving an organization in the direction of change without clarity about climate and culture, the leader risks alienating a portion of the constituency he or she serves. It is important to ask the right questions about why the organization, and more importantly, the people behave in ways marked by their words and actions. Gaining this insight is cornerstone to devising sustainable and collaborative plans to improve learning outcomes for students.

To be successful in their relationship, the board and the superintendent have to know their nonnegotiables: those elements that regardless of the situation or audience, they will continue to present as valuable. When a superintendency or situations borne from this leadership role begin to erode an internalized value structure, it may be time to move along and stake out a new claim, or engage those in the board–superintendent relationship in a genuine conversation to reach an acceptable collaborative compromise.

Good leaders find and cultivate opportunities for trust to form among the governance team. This is not always easy. Sometimes individuals on a team have loyalties to previous leaders or management styles, and regardless of the superintendent's efforts as a leader, those folks can be immovable. Balancing theory with action to formulate agency within teams in school districts requires additional nuances and tactics.

The superintendent cannot possibly lead until he or she intrinsically knows what he or she stands for. The politics, the power, the internalized culture, all have a way of creeping up and overpowering the virtues of the superintendent's best intentions. If the vision is clear, the identity for the work is established. The next critical elements are derived from a sustainability of that belief system when tested and challenged.

School board members and superintendents often bring their whole-self to the table, their sense of being and good worth. They also carry the knowledge and skills of the many people with whom they have crossed paths. This has helped them incorporate those language patterns and mannerisms to their confidence in delivering this part of the community's thinking at the board table. It is the superintendent's task to adopt and understand how these viewpoints affect their service to all constituents.

In working together, the board and the superintendent can quickly learn how they will operate with action steps linked to aspirational goals and vision. As a result, integrity in the board–superintendent relationship becomes examined through the perception of others. Both parties should present as genuine in their belief structure and decision-making practices. Actions should not be taken because they are politically expedient, but rather because they are forged out of shared experiences and tied to true standards and value judgments.

Judgment is a compelling barrier toward fomenting change in an organization: judgment not only in the sense of the value of an idea or innovation, but judgment in terms of the larger framework of an organization. In contemplating changes, first, one must construct or adopt a story based in reality. If however, the new district leader encounters a narrative of high-level district accomplishments that is not valid, the board and the school community may have already established a collective judgment, and therefore new thoughts and ideas may not be readily embraced.

Sometimes board members or the superintendent propose an outlandish idea to get a sensible middle. At other times, there is an attempt by the superintendent or board trustees to integrate unconventional ideas into a larger proposal to move these ideas forward with minimal scrutiny. Neither of these strategies is marked by integrity and can risk breaching the board–superintendent relationship. Risk brings both rewards and hazards, and therefore it takes time to deliberately refine the work to know exactly how to implement calculated uncertainties into the art of leadership.

No board–superintendent relationship is ever operationally whole. There are inherent gaps and blind spots that bespeckle the leadership landscape. This is particularly due to the obvious disparity in the committed hours that the superintendent must devote to supervising the district's daily operations as opposed to the board's tiered governance duties. The void between vision fueled by passion, integrity, and defined risk, is filled in by experience and practice.

Time and situational awareness bring with them the most powerful lessons. Theory is only effective as a guide, operationalizing action plans bring implementation to life. The span of any leadership position can promote proven insight where the superintendent learns to balance the theoretical with the practical to combine elements of the vision into larger schema. The key to this synergy is embracing the hope that is found in the collective aspirations that a school district engenders.

Every school community has rhythms that can sway the beat of progressive ideas and move the school district in new directions. As a district leader, it is important to become learned about differences in what the community expects versus the district's needs, and then use that knowledge to assess the ability of the school board to find common ground in that conversation. The superintendent's ability to communicate and bridge what may become divisive will be a determining factor in how the evaluation process unfolds.

Leadership is more than a series of words attached to actions. Leadership is the willingness, even at personal risk, to at first stand alone and attempt to shift the culture toward something of enhanced value and worth. Sometimes it is up to the leader to set the context for the debate rather than embracing the existing state of affairs. When this is pursued without deliberate care to culture and tradition, the evaluation feedback may not be what the superintendent ultimately expects.

Change cannot be immediately foisted upon a district. It is an evolution that must be developed, cultivated, and executed. Clean data that is examined through multiple perspectives communicates a compelling narrative. This is a critical component to ensure that multiple stakeholders commit to the change that the leader is seeking to actualize. This work requires grit and endurance and can take extensive periods of time to bring to fruition.

Simply having data and a strong argument may not be enough to end the disparate opinions surrounding an issue. An effective leader will bring their whole sense of personal efficacy to the proposal. It is that whole-self action coupled with the ability to effectively define the situation that clearly promotes the necessary elements of change. Furthermore to advance the goals and priorities of a district, the leader is ever watchful for a decline in the level of success momentum.

Consider how school district leaders are framed in the minds of people who work in schools. District leaders can be pigeonholed as the technology superintendent, the professional learning community (PLC) principal, the salesman, the hatchet person, the builder, or the consolidator. The initiatives that a superintendent brings to the district can anchor the perceptions of the school community and be both beneficial and detrimental.

For example, a new superintendent enters the district with much professional knowledge and expertise in the area of special education. This mastery level of best practices associated with serving special needs children will not be enough to ultimately realize a significant shift in the instructional delivery systems associated with this group of students. The superintendent must willfully and continuously connect the undergirding vision and mission of the district to focus on how the service to this student group is tied to overarching equity and inclusion goals. A technology superintendent will most likely implement technology goals, and a PLC principal will attempt to build PLC structures within the district. However, the efficacy and application of these initiatives within a school district are greatly dependent upon the engagement of the organization membership. This awareness must be actualized by a leader in order to effectively implement longitudinal goals.

As an experienced school district leader, solutions to a hindrance or roadblock that imperils student success can become immediately apparent. However, outlining the problem—and relative strategies—can involve the need for deep systemic improvement. School districts are not malleable and often resist today's rapid pace of change or transition. Transformational leaders serve with fidelity to the vision, but also listen, acknowledge, support, and at times cajole folks into attempting to see a different set of attainable outcomes. The role of leadership then is to continuously reframe the needs of the district along the spectrum of limitations and potential for growth.

Change will not spontaneously occur in most situations, and like watching a plant grow, it requires thoughtful cultivation. A strong communication plan coupled with purposeful dedication may still lead to unintended outcomes. Without careful consideration to all of the variables presented by the change process and feedback from multiple perspectives, the superintendent's evaluation process can become corrupted by pitfalls along the way.

There are many times along the journey of educational leadership that the superintendent finds their ideas radicalized as a result of poor implementation. The vision of a particular programmatic shift is borne from the partnership between the superintendent and the board of education. However, if there are not checkpoints and communication loops through which the next level of management must vet their creativity, before the superintendent can "right the ship," the original idea can become an animal of a different breed or so cumbersome that it fails to achieve its long-term objectives.

In considering this, the mastery of the superintendent's vision or idea circulates back to the board–superintendent relationship. As a reflective leader, the superintendent will know when to convey to the board that it is necessary to pivot and recalibrate to safeguard their shared ideas to realize the successful implementation of district goals. This is not a skillset that superintendents necessarily possess at the beginning of their tenure as leaders. However, such expertise may emerge as time and situations allow for district leaders to learn and grow.

Consequently, the takeaway is that when an idea does not unfold the way a leader anticipates, he or she should be prepared to regroup, and reorganize their coalition and goals. The improvement of the leader's communication and engagement of others in the topic will then drive the future conversational narrative. In education, as in any industry, timing and knowing the consumers is critical. Implementing strategic reforms bring with them both risk and reward.

But there is profound value to mastery, to confidence, to knowing limits and audience, to being purposeful and joyful, that brings the essential elements of eliciting change forward when a board and a superintendent are operating from a common vision. Knowing that at times the board–superintendent relationship will not always go as anticipated means the partnership must be operationalized to be able to effectively adapt to changing conditions as they unfold.

Leadership is about finding the significance in what others value. Worthy initiatives reflect more than the immediacies of the moment and create a sustainable vision for systemic change. The superintendent can find success in enterprises that are strategically aligned to the espoused philosophies of a district. However, the superintendent will often encounter challenges that will be evident in how a board views the work product of the superintendent if this does not ring true.

A new superintendent is eager to get to work building a strategic vision for the future of the district. After assessing the state of the district as part of the entry period, the superintendent begins to "seed the clouds" with board members by providing them with information relating to a host of topics ranging from the rate of students' summer reading regression to a rising special education identification rate to the organization of contemporary learning spaces. To fortify the perception of his role as the instructional leader of the district, the superintendent pursues building the background knowledge of board members by providing articles from professional journals, trade publications, and anecdotes from other area districts in his weekly update. The list of attachments grows longer each passing week as the superintendent organizes the reference material that he hopes will aid the board in conceptualizing the various areas identified in the entry period as needing attention.

As the weeks go by, the superintendent finds more articles and sends them along, waiting for the moment to bring all of the thinking together with the board to get their perspectives on the work ahead. Before this can happen, board members begin to question why they are getting so many articles, how there could be this many things needing improvement, and just what all of these seemingly random areas of focus had to do with a vision and the success momentum for the district.

The superintendent soon realized the thinking behind the sharing of the information was not communicated well. In fact, the superintendent had not taken the board on the intended intellectual journey, he had merely flooded their inboxes with disjointed articles. The vision he wished to articulate was not being constructed with the board in a collaborative way. The superintendent now understood he had created a problem of his own making. Some board members wanted to begin work on all of the identified action areas, others were offended that the superintendent believed that this many items were in need of review, and still others were questioning how these documents related to policy and budget development, the expressed purview of the board. The superintendent wrote the following note to the board after a fairly intense conversation about strategic planning at a recent meeting with them:

> I am sincerely appreciative of our dialog during last night's board meeting and there are a few variables upon which I must reflect. First, I must better frame and organize my communication with the board as we only formally meet twice a month. I realize that I got swept up in my excitement to move an agenda that I've intimately studied and am impassioned to move forward.
> I called my mentor who reminded me that the superintendency must be treated as a sprint not a marathon, and knowing when to run faster is the part of the opportunity for me to grow as a leader. Second, in trying to stick to a "no surprise rule," I have failed to adequately build a comprehensive narrative that you can reference as we discuss this work in the coming months. I plan to double down on my efforts to sequence information sharing so that you more easily recognize the development of ideas. This should avoid the kind of confusion evident in our last meeting.
>
> I know you are all extremely busy and this is my full time job. I will keep working to find a more effective way of outlining the work ahead while simultaneously laying the necessary groundwork on a multitude of topics. Much of what I am giving you is like planting seeds, you plant them, and in some cases, the plant takes weeks, months, or years to come to fruition; but you have to plant them for anything to happen. I will be more deliberate in defining the timeframes for "sprouting seeds."
>
> Building a vision with you, and identifying supportive resources in our school budget, will define my opening years with this organization. This has been the quintessential misstep in this district for the last decade. As difficult as it is to state outright, this is the reason why I have been compelled to plant so many seeds. You have the resources within our school budget; however, they have not been aligned with the needs of this school community. Saying this out loud is a courageous step for me as there is much at stake. However, without building from this honest foundation, and without these seeds planted, our shared deliverables will be diminished.
>
> I need all of you. I do not want to alienate any of you. I came here because of you. I will work as hard as I can to better prioritize of all of the initiatives that I believe we should pursue. I need and value your partnership as leaders of this community to gain a better sense of where you want to go. We can do this work together and I want you to know that I heard you. Hang in there with me.

The superintendent had to hit the "reset button" with the board very early on in his tenure. In not orienting his actions with the board, but rather foisting findings on them in the form of exemplars of how things should be, the superintendent became isolated, created mountains of work, lost time in building on previous successes, and expended some political capital that a new leader had yet to really build up with a school board. All of this impacted how he was perceived, whether he was in too deep, and whether, just maybe, irreparable damage was done to the fledgling relationship with the board.

The construction of the vision without clear communication and shared understandings is a perilous task and there are multiple missteps that can occur along the way. If the board is not clear on what they want, why they want it, and how they got to that thinking with each other, then the vision, despite its grammatical clarity will continue to be murky and this confusion will be evinced in the superintendent's evaluation as a byproduct of board members' disparate perspectives.

Because the evaluation is inevitable, all parties should engage in some collaborative time to suss out understandings and devise communication protocols that enhance teamwork among the members of the board and the superintendent. This will eliminate ambiguity about why specific action steps are being implemented and the impact of these efforts throughout the district.

Communication protocols such as the ones outlined below organize the flow of information ensuring that opportunities for problem solving are evenly distributed among all members of the governing board. This strengthens the working board–superintendent relationship and builds organizational systems that culminate in consistent responses to constituent inquiries.

COMMUNICATION PROTOCOLS

1. Surprises to the board or the superintendent should not occur. We agree to ask the board president to place an item on the agenda as opposed to bringing it up unexpectedly at the meeting.
2. Conduct at a board meeting is very important. We agree to avoid words and actions that create a negative impression on an individual, the board, or the district. While we encourage debate and differing points of view, we will do it with care and respect to avoid an escalation of negative impressions or incidents.

3. To be efficient and effective, extending board meetings should be avoided when possible. During a board meeting, if a board member believes he or she does not have enough information or has questions, the board should consider tabling the agenda item.
4. Regular board meetings are for decision making, action, and votes, not endless discussion. We agree to "move the questions" when discussion is repetitive.
5. The board will not play to the audience. We agree to speak to the issues on the agenda and attend to our fellow board members. Facts and information needed from the administration will be referred to the superintendent.
6. Communication between the superintendent and the board is encouraged. However, board information sharing and/or requests that will require time, action, or have political implications are to be directed to the superintendent and the board president and include the full board for discussion.
7. All personnel questions or concerns received by the board or its individual members will be directed to the superintendent.
8. The last stop, not the first, will be to the board. We agree to follow the chain of command and insist that others attend to this standard operating practice.
9. The superintendent, as the CEO, and/or the board president are the spokesperson(s) for the district. All community concerns and/or issues received by the board and individual board members should be directed to the superintendent.
10. Individual board members do not have authority. Only the board as a whole has authority.
11. Electronic communication should be concise and respectful.
12. In the case of emergency situations, the superintendent's initial contact will be with the board president and action will be taken regarding immediate communication with the rest of the board.

Once a vision is established, it is the responsibility of the superintendent to publicize the action steps that target achievement of the stated goal(s). It is also important for the board president to work with the superintendent to build a schedule of presentations that engages the board, administration, and other critical stakeholder groups including students in an ongoing dialogue about the implementation of action steps that ultimately match the vision of the district with what is actually happening in schools and classrooms. An example is shown in table 5.1.

Waiting until the end of the year to reflect on the work hinders both the efficacy with which goals can be accomplished and the success momentum of the board–superintendent relationship. The responsibility for advancing the work of the district is found in this dynamic and without a predetermined presentation schedule, the final evaluation will become more of a listing of what folks felt could have been done or improved upon rather than a growth document that sustains successful leadership practices and works to improve upon those skills in need of additional refinement.

The quality of the evaluation speaks to the virtues of the process derived to create it. The process utilized in creating the evaluation is influenced by the values a board and superintendent, through their relationship, place upon it. If the evaluation is valuable to the board as an operative tool, because there is an espoused philosophy as to what it means, comprehensive feedback by board members into the process will produce a document that has substance.

If the evaluation is viewed more broadly as a contractual chore that is hastily completed, it will become less viable in its usefulness to the district and the superintendent. If the practice of regular engagement in the evaluation process does not occur, superintendents can forgo the collection of data that strengthens the professional performance of district leadership. In the end, boards will mute the development of real goals and the projected vision will lack substance and meaningful input.

If the board–superintendent relationship is upended by electoral consequences, the absence of a robust evaluation process can negatively impact contract negotiations and renewal. On the other hand, if the superintendent seeks feedback, and the board views the evaluation as something that is not critical, the superintendent could begin to feel as though there is a lack of value placed by the board members on the work that the superintendent is doing. Consequently, this dynamic can erode the relationship even if everything else is going well on the surface.

Evaluations are as much about the past as they are the future. Because the experiences of the evaluators are informed by previous practice, and the events that they are being asked to render judgment have transpired throughout the school year, making the evaluation about the future requires a vision that speaks to aspirational claims for a school district. This methodology requires a relational bond between the board and the superintendent where

Table 5.1. Sample vision action step calendar.

Board presentation	Presentation topic	Person or people presenting
September board meeting	Summer school report, security update, coteaching initiatives	Summer school principal, superintendent, assistant superintendents for special services and curriculum and instruction
October board meeting	Strategic plan update, overview of new state learning standards, board of education recognition	Superintendent, assistant superintendent for curriculum and instruction, students/staff across the district
November board meeting	Bond update, instructional coaching program	Construction management company, assistant superintendent for curriculum and instruction
December board meeting	Board of education recognition program, guidance and mental health programs	Superintendent, assistant superintendents for student services and curriculum and instruction
January board meeting	District technology update, English as a new language program (presentation from students)	Director of technology, assistant superintendent for special services
February board meeting	Science program update (focus on environmentally friendly activities with presentation from students)	Assistant superintendent for curriculum and instruction
March board meeting	Two principals' annual reports, budget presentation	Principals, superintendent/assistant, superintendent for business
April board meeting	Board of education recognition program, two principals' annual reports	Superintendent, principals
May board meeting	District technology update, strategic plan update	Director of technology, superintendent
June board meeting	Year-end celebrations: retirements, tenure, empire games	Superintendent/other administrators, assistant superintendent for special services

actively leading for the future is not only part of the evaluation, but overall the work of the district.

It is all too easy to become mired in the everyday experiences of running a school district and forget to lay claim to a future for the district. Moving away from the administrative duties involved in running a district toward a more authentic engagement of envisioning the challenges of the future demands that the narrative about what a district hopes to achieve be more than superficial, and is embedded in the superintendent's evaluation process.

To advance, the school district's espoused philosophy has to expand beyond the perfunctory and be part of something that sets out to improve learning conditions for educators and students. The same expectation must also be present in the evaluation of its leader. It must go beyond checklists, and build into an ongoing and intentional process that advances the work of the district, and helps the superintendent build his or her capacity to become a reflective practitioner.

In the end, what matters is that the superintendent's evaluation process is borne from a deliberative effort on both sides of the board–superintendent relationship. Leaving the evaluation to a last minute—as a year-end action step—shortchanges all the parties. Communication, and the articulation of areas of the superintendent's success as well as areas for improvement, each help to build and sustain the board–superintendent partnership. This partnership grows and is developed over time with input from stakeholders to the evaluation process.

The ability of a superintendent to be responsive to the needs of a board without constructive feedback is complicated and lacks transparency. Without meaningful dialogue with the leader, how can these community-elected representatives evaluate the progress of the initiatives that help tell the district's continuous improvement story?

School superintendent evaluation is not a straightforward proposition. This is supported by the increasing dependence on checklists and rubric-driven evaluation tools that have been mutually adopted by boards and superintendents across the country. The landscape of education is continually being redrawn, increasing the demands on existing educational systems. Relying on what has always been done without examining the "why" of the process and "what" the board and superintendent hope to get out of the evaluation only placates the cyclical calendar of evaluation requirements without focusing the vision and corresponding action steps necessary to achieve a meaningful growth.

As Eleanor Roosevelt once said, "the way to begin is to begin," and without taking that first step, the process will remain largely static until there is an outside force that causes a disruption. Even the most incremental action serves to generate success momentum.

Epilogue

Evaluating the Superintendent

As someone who served as a superintendent for twenty-seven years, I know firsthand just how difficult the job is, and how rewarding it can be.

I was surprised that some of my friends thought my job followed the "school schedule" with summers off. Nothing could be further from the truth. A superintendent's job is 24/7, 365 days a year. Adding today's technology into the mix makes the superintendent always on call. Long hours come with the package.

The superintendent must become a powerful political figure within the community. Being politically active is essential to thriving and surviving. The first step in that direction is community engagement. The superintendent must be out and about, meeting and greeting constituents and educating them about district priorities and successes.

Visibility is paramount. The media is a powerful ally in this effort. Rather than ducking from reporters, the superintendent must seek them out. Social media is another powerful tool to engage with the wider community.

To best serve the more than fifty million children learning and growing in our public schools, our school system leaders must possess a growing set of skills and knowledge and a robust professional network. The success of the district chief has a direct impact on the school district itself, the students in the school buildings, and the neighborhoods where our young learners reside.

Whether you are an aspiring superintendent, one who has been on the job for two years or twenty, I recommend *Evaluating the Superintendent* by

Connie Evelyn and Jarett Powers. This resource provides a myriad of practical strategies about fostering a healthy relationship between the superintendent and the school board. The authors explore why a positive working relationship with members of the school board can never be underestimated.

As I travel across the country, I hear time and time again from superintendents and other administrators who say, "We can't do it alone." That is why creating effective professional networks comprise a major linchpin to success. With that in mind, the single-most important network a superintendent needs to establish is with the school board.

My good friend, Tom Gentzel, the executive director of the National School Boards Association, and I have an annual session during our national conferences where we each provide a perspective from our vantage point on the education issues of the day. We both agree that in this era of accountability, the superintendent and the school board must be in lock step with each other.

I am of the same opinion as Evelyn and Powers, who point out that "an informed perspective regarding the functions and purpose of a governing board has a significant impact on understanding the capacity of the role of the superintendent." Accordingly, I would recommend that superintendents, particularly new superintendents, read *Evaluating the Superintendent*. It is insightful and useful.

—Daniel A. Domenech, executive director
American Association of School Administrators

References

Abrams, J. (1987). The best lessons I've learned as a superintendent. *The Executive Educator, 9*(3), 20–21.

Akenhead, J. (1984). Size up your superintendent's "style." *American School Board Journal, 171*(10), 32–33, 42.

Bagin, D., Gallagher, D. R., & Moore, E. (2008). *The school and community relations*. Boston: Pearson/Allyn & Bacon.

Banks, P. A., & Maloney, R. J. (2007). Changing the subject of your evaluation. *School Administrator, 64*(6).

Bippus, S. (1985). A full, fair, and formal evaluation will enable your superintendent to excel. *American School Board Journal, 172*(4), 42–43.

Bjork, L. G. (1993). Effective schools-effective superintendents: The emerging instructional leadership role. *Journal of School Leadership, 3*(3), 246–259.

Blumberg, A. (1985). A superintendent must read the board's invisible job description. *American School Board Journal, 172*(9), 44–45.

Bolman, L. G., & Deal, T. E. (2003). *Reframing organizations artistry, choice, and leadership*. San Francisco: John Wiley & Sons, Inc.

Booth, R., & Glaub, G. (1978). Planned appraisal of the superintendent. A performance based program for school boards and superintendents. A handbook. *Illinois association of school boards*, 3–88.

Boring, M. (2011). Superintendent search. *Washington State School Directors' Association Superintendent Search Handbook*.

Boyd, J. (1966). How to appraise school superintendents. *The Nation's Schools, 78*, 34–38.

Braddom, C. (1986). Prescription for improvement: make certain your school board's system of evaluating the superintendent is fair, fast, factual, and frequent. *American School Board Journal, 173*(8), 28–29.

Bridges, W. (2009). *Managing transitions* (3rd ed.). Philadelphia: Da Capo Press.

Brodinski, B. (1983). Boards and superintendents: How to have a healthy relationship. *Updating School Board Policies, 14*(2).

Calzi, F., & Heller, R. (1989). Make evaluation the key to your superintendent's success. *American School Board Journal, 176*(4), 33–34.

Candoli, I., Cullen, K., & Stufflebeam, D. (1997). *Superintendent performance evaluation: Current practice and directions for improvement*. Boston: Kluwer Academic.

Carol, L. (1972). Study of methods for evaluating chief school officers in local school districts. *New Jersey School Boards Association*, 1–56.

Carver, J. (2006). *Boards that make a difference: A new design for leadership in nonprofit and public organizations* (3rd ed.). San Francisco: Jossey-Bass.

Castallo, R. (1999). Superintendent evaluation. *American School Board Journal, 186*(8), 23–26.

Castallo, R., Greco, J., & McGowan, T. (1992). Clear signals. *American School Board Journal, 179*(2), 32–34.

Center for Educational Leadership. (2015). 4 dimensions of instructional leadership. Retrieved July 30, 2017, from https://www.k-12leadership.org/content/service/4-dimensions-instructional-leadership.

Chand, K. (1984). Evaluation of superintendents. *Resources in Education* (ERIC Document Reproduction Service No. ED 245 341), 1–14.

Chingos, M. M., Whitehurst, G. J., & Lindquist, K. M. (2014, September 3). *School superintendents: Vital or irrelevant*. Washington, DC: Brookings Institution, 77–95.

Clear, D. (1983). Our superintendent is succeeding because we told her what we want. *American School Board Journal, 170*(70), 29, 38.

Crew, R. (2007). *Only connect: The way to save our schools*. New York: Farrar, Straus and Giroux.

Cuban, L. (1977). Why not tell the superintendent what you think of him . . . at least twice a year? *Updating School Board Policies*.

Davidson, J. L. (1970). *Effective school board meetings*. West Nyack, NY: Parker Pub. Co.

Dervarics, C., & O'Brien, E. (2011). Eight characteristics of effective school boards: Full report. *Center for Public Education*.

Dickinson, D. (1980). Superintendent evaluation requires a sophisticated, step-by-step plan like the one you'll find right here. *American School Board Journal, 167*(6), 34–38.

Dillon, R., & Halliwell, J. (1991). Superintendents' and school board presidents' perceptions of the purposes, strengths and weaknesses of formal superintendent evaluations. *Journal of School Leadership, 1*, 328–337.

DiPaola, M. (2010). *Evaluating the superintendent* [White paper]. Retrieved September 29, 2017, from http://www.aasa.org/uploadedFiles/Resources/AASA_White_Paper_on_Superintendent_Evaluation.pdf.

DiPaola, M., & Stronge, J. H. (2003). *Superintendent evaluation handbook*. Lanham, MD: Scarecrow Press.

Dittloff, R. (1982). Evaluate the superintendent. *Evaluate the Superintendent, 169*(11), 41.

Dykes, A. R. (1965). *School board and superintendent: Their effective working relationships*. Danville, IL: Interstate Printers & Publishers.

Eadie, D. (2003). High impact governing. *American School Board Journal, 190*(7), 26–29.

Edwards, M. (1988). Setting school board goals: A model for accountability. *Educational Horizons, 66*(3), 117–118.

Ehrenberg, R. G., Chaykowski, R. P., & Ehrenberg, R. A. (1988). Are school superintendents rewarded for "performance"? [Electronic version]. In D. Monk (Ed.), *Microlevel school finance: Issues and implications for policy* (pp. 337–364). Cambridge, MA: Ballinger Publishing.

Evans, R. (1996). *The human side of school change: Reform, resistance, and the real-life problems of innovation*. San Francisco: Jossey-Bass.

References

Evelyn, C. (2012). Board of education and superintendent operating communication protocols. Auburn, NY.

First, P. (1990). How to effectively evaluate a superintendent. *Thrust for Educational Leadership*, *21*(3), 40–44.

Fitzwater, I. (1973). How does your superintendent rate? Questions that will help you give an answer. *School Management*, 26.

Foldesy, G. (1989). *Developing policy on evaluation and assessment of school board and superintendent performance* (pp. 1–31). Tuscaloosa, AL.

Fowler, C. (1977). Why superintendents fail. *American School Board Journal*, *64*(2), 21–23.

Freund, S. A. (1988). Superintendent: Here's how I stay friends with the board president. *American School Board Journal*, *175*(6), 39.

Fulbright, L. & Goodman, R. H. (1999). Ten things superintendents can do to create and maintain an effective school governance team. *ERS Spectrum*, *17*(4), 3–13.

Glass, T. E., Brunner, C. C., & Bjork, L. (2000). *The study of the American school superintendency, 2000. A look at the superintendent of education in the new millennium*. Arlington, VA: American Association of School Administrators.

Glaub, G. (1983). Board and superintendent share appraisal benefits. *Updating School Board Policies*, *14*(4).

Grady, M., & Bryant, M. (1991). School board presidents tell why their superintendents fail. *The Executive Educator*, *13*(5), 24–25.

Hallinger, P. (2003). Leading educational change: Reflections on the practice of instructional and transformational leadership. *Cambridge Journal of Education*, *33*(3), 329–351.

Hallinger, P., & Murphy, J. (1986). The superintendent as instructional leader: Findings from effective school districts. *Journal of Educational Administration*, *24*(2), 213–236.

Hawkins, W. (1972). Performance evaluation: Starting with the superintendent. *Thrust for Educational Leadership*, (1).

Hawley, W. D. (1994). Seeking the essential superintendent. *School Administrator*, *51*(7), 32–33.

Hayden, J. (1986). Crisis at the helm. *The School Administrator*, *43*(10), 17–19.

Heller, R. W. (1978). *Superintendent evaluation* (pp. 1–25). Anaheim, CA.

Hendricks, S. (2013). Evaluating the superintendent: The role of the school board. *Education Leadership Review*, *14*(3), 62–72.

Henrikson, R. (2018). Superintendent evaluation frameworks for continuous improvement: Using evidence-based processes to promote the stance of improvement. *AASA Journal of Scholarship and Practice*, *15*(1), 22–29.

Horn, J. D. (1996). *The evaluation role of school boards: A superintendent's perspective*. Kalamazoo, MI: Educational Resources Information Center.

Houston, P., & Eadie, D. (2002). *The board-savvy superintendent*. Lanham, MD: Scarecrow Press.

Hoy, W., & Miskel, C. (2008). *Educational administration: Theory, research, and practice* (8th ed.). Boston: McGraw-Hill.

Hoyle, J. R. (1993). *Professional standards for the superintendency*. Lanham, MD: R&L Education.

Hoyle, J. R., & Skrla, L. (1999). The politics of superintendent evaluation. *Journal of Personnel Evaluation in Education*, *13*(4), 405–419.

Jentz, B. C., & Murphy, J. T. (2005). Starting confused: How leaders start when they don't know where to start. *Phi Delta Kappan*, *86*(10), 736–744.

Jernigan, S. (1997). Dangerous expectations: why a superintendent search often breeds discontent and unsatisfying results. *School Administrator*, 54(2), 8.

Jones, J. (1981, April). There's more to the evaluation of a superintendent than meets the eye. Paper presented at annual meeting of the National School Boards Association, Dallas, Texas.

Jones, R. (1994). Worth his weight? *American School Board Journal, 181*(12), 30–32.

Kalkhoven, S. (1981, April). Effective superintendent evaluation—it's not that difficult. Paper presented at annual meeting of the National School Boards Association, Dallas, Texas.

Katz, M. (1993). Matching school board and superintendent styles. *School Administrator, 50*(2).

Kibby, G. (1965). How to evaluate your superintendent. *School Management* (9), 42–45.

Konnert, M. W., & Augenstein J. J. (1990). *The superintendency in the nineties: What superintendents and board members need to know*. Lancaster, PA: Technomic Publishing Company, Inc.

Kotter, J. P. (1996). *Leading change*. Boston: Harvard Business Review.

Kowalski, T. (1998). Critiquing the CEO evaluation. *American School Board Journal, 185*(2), 43–44.

Kowalski, T. (2005). *The school superintendent: Theory, practice, and cases*. Thousand Oaks, CA: Sage Publications.

Lewis, E. L. (Ed.). (1975). Guidelines for evaluating a superintendent. *California School Boards Association*.

Lindgren, J. (1985). Evaluating your superintendent. *California School Boards Association*.

Luehe, B. (1989). Fine-tuning keeps board/superintendent relations on track and running smoothly. *American School Board Journal, 176*(10), 33–42.

Martin, J. A., & Martin, R. H. (1992). Board members: Informing them begins with knowing who they are. *Journal of School Leadership, 2*(4), 419–428.

Mathews, J. (2001). The tenuous nature of superintendent evaluation. *School Administrator, 58*(2), 6–8.

Mayo, C., & McCartney, G. P. (2004). School superintendents' evaluations: effective and results-based? *Spectrum: Journal of School Research and Information, 22*(1), 19–33.

McCarty, D. (1971). Evaluating your superintendent. *School Management, 15*(7), 38–39.

McCurdy, J., & Hymes, D. L. (1992). *Building better board-administrator relations. An AASA critical issues report*. Arlington, VA: American Association of School Administrators.

Mitchell, B. (1994). Set fair rules and stick to them. *American School Board Journal, 181*(12), 32–33.

Mountford, M. (2004). Motives and power of school board members: Implications for school board-superintendent relationships. *Educational Administration Quarterly, 40*(5), 704–741.

National Policy Board for Educational Administration. (2015). Professional standards for educational leaders 2015. Reston, VA.

O'Hara, D. G. (1994). The superintendent's first contract. *School Administrator, 51*(7), 19–21.

Ornstein, A. (1990). Superintendents: gauge your performance and productivity. *The Executive Educator, 12*(8), 22–25.

Pajak, E. F., & Glickman, C. D. (1989). Dimensions of school district improvement. *Educational Leadership, 46*(8), 61–64

Patterson, J. (2000). *The anguish of leadership*. Arlington, VA: American Association of School Administrators.

Patterson, J. (2003). *Coming even cleaner about organizational change*. Lanham, MD: Scarecrow Press.

Pitner, N. J., & Ogawa, R. T. (1981). Organizational leadership: The case of the school superintendent. *Educational Administration Quarterly, 17*(2), 45–65.

Portis, C, & Garcia, M. W. (2007). Superintendent as change leader. *The School Administrator, 64*(3), 18–27.

Powers, J. (2017). Publicly available information regarding the evaluation of school district superintendents in New York State. *ProQuest LLC*.

Ramirez, A., & Guzman, N. (2003). The superintendent search: An analysis of ISLCC standards compared to school board developed selection criteria. *Education Leadership Review, 4*(2), 34–37.

Richardson, M. D., Lane, K. E., & Flanigan, J. L. (1996). Teachers' perceptions of principals' attributes. *The Clearing House, 69*, 290–292.

Robinson, G. E., & Bickers, P. M. (1990). *Evaluation of superintendents and school boards*. Arlington, VA: Educational Research Service.

Roelle, R., & Monks, R. (1978). A six-point plan for evaluating your superintendent. *American School Board Journal, 165*(9), 36–37.

Sabatino, A. J. (2010). Hiring a superintendent: What school boards want. Retrieved from http://library.sage.edu:2048/login?url=http://search.proquest.com/docview/763195757?account=13645.

Salley, C. (1980). Superintendents' job priorities. *Administrator's Notebook, 28*(1), 1–4.

Schein, E. H. (1996). Culture: The missing concept in organization studies. *Administrative Science Quarterly, 41*(2), 229–240.

Schmitz, S. A., & Fitch, L. A. (2001). Leadership intoxication: Recognize the seduction of power before it costs you your job. *American School Board Journal, 188*(1), 44–45.

Shannon, T. A. (1989). What a superintendent can do about conflict with the school board. *American School Board Journal, 176*(6), 25–27.

Smoley, E. R., Jr. (1999). *Effective school boards: Strategies for improving board performance. The Jossey-Bass Education Series*. San Francisco: Jossey-Bass.

Stronge, J. H. (1998). Leadership skills in school and business. *School Administrator, 55*(9), 21–24, 26.

Swain, P. (1975). How board members evaluate the superintendent. Paper presented at American Association of School Administrators annual convention, Dallas, Texas.

Tallerico, M. (1989). The dynamics of superintendent–school board relationships. *Urban Education, 24*(2), 215–232.

Tallerico, M. (2000). Gaining access to the superintendency: Headhunting, gender, and color. *Educational Administration Quarterly, 36*(1), 18–43.

Thomas, M. D. (1975). Partner of the board. The board/superintendent relationship. *California School Boards, 34*(3), 4–6.

Turner, L. L. (1971). Your superintendent: When to recharge him—or discharge him. *American School Board Journal, 159*(1), 16–19.

Waters, J. T., & Marzano, R. J. (2006). School district leadership that works: The effect of superintendent leadership on student achievement.

About the Authors

Constance D. Evelyn has been the superintendent of schools for the Valley Stream Thirteen UFSD since 2015 and has held leadership positions. In her more than twenty-five years of experience as an educator, she has been a superintendent in two districts; assistant superintendent; elementary and middle school principal; and prekindergarten, middle, and high school teacher. As a longtime public educator, Evelyn has received numerous awards and recognition for her leadership, including the passage of a New York legislative resolution recognizing her dedication and service to students across the state. As a superintendent, she was twice appointed by the governor's office to serve on influential committees focused on state learning standards and the allocation of resources for technology in schools. She has a BA in psychology from the College of Staten Island and two degrees from Long Island University (education and educational leadership), and she earned her doctorate in education leadership from the Sage Colleges.

Jarett Powers has been superintendent of the Union Springs Central School District in Union Springs, New York, since November 2014. Prior to working in Union Springs, Powers was principal of Ithaca High School, associate principal of Ithaca High School, and Social Studies Department chair. He earned three degrees in education and educational leadership from SUNY Cortland and holds a BA from Ithaca College in social studies education, and he earned his doctorate in educational leadership from the Sage Colleges.

www.ingramcontent.com/pod-product-compliance
Lightning Source LLC
Chambersburg PA
CBHW030145240426
43672CB00005B/278